DICTIONARY OF ASTROLOGY

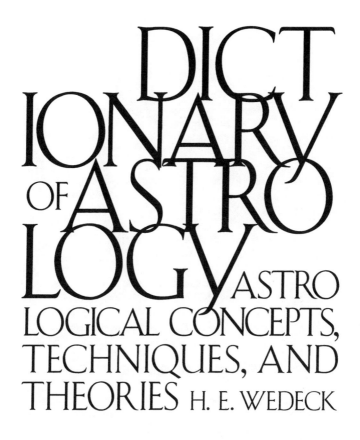

DICTIONARY OF ASTROLOGY

ASTROLOGICAL CONCEPTS, TECHNIQUES, AND THEORIES

H. E. WEDECK

A Citadel Press Book
Published by Carol Publishing Group

Carol Publishing Group Edition, 1995

Previously published as *Dictionary of Astrology*

A Citadel Press Book
Published by Carol Publishing Group
Citadel Press is a registered trademark of Carol Communications, Inc.

Editorial Offices: 600 Madison Avenue, New York, NY 10022
Sales & Distribution Offices: 120 Enterprise Avenue, Secaucus, NJ 07094
In Canada: Canadian Manda Group, One Atlantic Avenue, Suite 105
Toronto, Ontario, M6K 3E7

Manufactured in the United States of America
10 9 8 7 6 5 4 3 2 1

Carol Publishing Group books are available at special discounts for bulk purchases, sales promotions, fund raising, or educational purposes. Special editions can be created to specifications. For details contact: Special Sales Department, Carol Publishing Group, 120 Enterprise Ave., Secaucus, NJ 07094

Library of Congress Cataloging-in-Publication Data

Wedeck, Harry Ezekiel, 1894-
        The dictionary of astrology : astrological concepts, techniques, and theories / H.E. Wedeck.
                p.   cm.
"A Citadel Press Book."
ISBN 8-8065-1712-3
1. Astrology—Dictionaries. I. Title.
BF1655.W4   1995   95-9360
133.5'03—dc20   CIP

INTRODUCTION

Astrology postulates a belief that the heavenly bodies govern and affect the course of human life. Whether it is considered a science, an art, or a pseudo-science, astrology has exerted a tremendous influence through the ages.

It was practiced in the ancient Greco-Roman world, in Egypt and Mesopotamia, in the Orient and in Africa and in Gaul. It was particularly in vogue in the Middle Ages, and at the present time it is again triumphant.

Astrology has touched all levels of society. It has attracted poets and merchants, philosophers and peasants, warriors and emperors, as well as the common man and his wife. Astrology has been gravely regarded as responsible for the fall of dynasties, for wars and revolutions, for earthquakes and massacres, for cosmic cataclysms and domestic bliss and misfortune.

In these contemporary, restless, and turbulent times, astrology has acquired a new lease on life. Once again, as in Roman imperial days, it has asserted its mysterious dominance over the minds of men.

This book defines the fundamental concepts of astrological lore and its technical aspects. It notes certain trends in its popularity, and it touches on personalities who have been drawn to astrological study as a possible means of interpreting the cycle of the cosmic scheme.

HEW

DICT
IONARY
OF ASTRO
LOGY

ABBEN-RAGEL

An Arabian astrologer, generally known by his Latinized name of Alchabitius. His treatise on astrology, published in the tenth century, was translated into Latin and printed in 1473, under the title of *De iudiciis seu fatis stellarum*. Many of his predictions were fulfilled.

ABENEZRA

(1092-1167) Jewish polymath and linguist, poet, traveler. Author of treatises on astrology, among them *De Nativitatibus*.

ABOU RYHAN

(Mohammed Ben Ahmed) An Arabian astrologer credited with introducing judicial astrology. He is assumed to have possessed to a remarkable degree the power to predict future events.

ABRAHAM

According to an ancient tradition, the patriarch Abraham was himself an astrologer.

ABRAHAM IBN EZRA

Medieval Jewish scholar and mathematician. Official astrologer to the court of Barcelona. Author of two astrological treatises: *Sentences of the Constellations* and *The Book of the World.*

ABRAHAM THE CHALDEAN
On his breast Abraham the Chaldean bore a large astrological tablet on which the fate of every man might be read. For this reason the kings of the East and the West congregated every morning, according to a tradition, in order to seek his advice.

ABSCISSION OR FRUSTRATION
When a planet is simultaneously forming an aspect to two other planets, the one that culminates first may produce an abscission of light that will frustrate the influence of the second aspect.

ACADEMIC RECOGNITION
In most of the medieval universities of Europe, particularly at Oxford, astrology, with which astronomy was closely linked, was among the disciplines that constituted the academic curriculum.

ACCIDENTAL ASCENDANT
A device employed by Evangeline Adams whereby to draw horary interpretations from a natal Figure. In applying this method one determines the Ascendant for the moment the question is propounded, and rotates the Figure until the degree occupies the East Point.

ACCURACY OF PREDICTIONS
In his *Tetrabiblos* Ptolemy asserts that if astrological predictions are incorrect, they are so not on account of any inherent astrological defect, but because the practitioners of the art are not sufficiently skilled in interpretation.

ACRONYCAL
This expression used in astrology stems from the Greek words that mean *in the edge of the night*. It is said of the rising after

2

sunset, or the setting before sunrise, of a planet that is in opposition to the Sun: hence in a favorable position for astronomical observation. Acronycal Place: the degree it will occupy when it is in opposition to the Sun.

ACTIVE INFLUENCE
The result of an aspect between two or more astrological factors or sensitive points, thereby producing the action that can materialize in an event.

ADAM
In the early Christian centuries there was tradition that Adam was knowledgeable in astrology.

ADAMS, EVANGELINE
This American astrologer, who died in 1932, was one of the most popular professionals. Her radio program appealed to hundreds of thousands of listeners. Among her clients she had J. P. Morgan the financier, Enrico Caruso, and King Edward VII.

ADJUSTED CALCULATION DATE
This term is used with reference to a directed or progressed horoscope, indicating the date on which the planet culminates. A variant term is Limiting Date.

ADOLESCENT
Adolescents born under the sign of Libra or Taurus experience the most tranquil period free from internal or external conflict.

ADVANTAGE, LINE OF
This term is used with reference to the position of the Moon's Ascending Node in a Geocentric Figure. The line of advantage runs between the cusps of the third decanates of the Third and Ninth Houses. A position of the Node East of this line is judged to be favorable. Related to it are the Arcs of Increased and Dwarfed Stature. From the middle of the First House, clockwise to the middle of the Eighth House, is the Arc of Increased Stature, with its peak at the cusp of the Twelfth House; and from the

Seventh House, clockwise to the middle of the Second House, is the Arc of Dwarfed Stature, with its peak at the cusp of the Sixth House.

AFFINITY
This astrological term denotes a binding by mutual attraction. The Sun is said to have an affinity with all the planets; Mars with Venus, in a magnetic or physical sense; Venus with Jupiter, in a philanthropic sense; Venus with Mercury, in an artistic sense.

AFFLICTED
An astrological term that means unfavorably aspected. The term is loosely applied to any inharmonious aspect to a planet, or to any aspect, particularly the conjunction, parallel, square, or opposition to a malefic planet. Some authorities apply the term to a mundane or zodiacal parallel or when besieged by both Infortunes. Again, the sensitive degree on any house cusp can be afflicted, though such consideration must be confined to instances where the birth-moment is known.

AIR SIGNS
These are Aquarius, Gemini, Libra.

ALBEDO
This astrological term means *whiteness*. It is a measure of the reflecting power of a planet, in ratio to its absorptive capacity, expressed in a figure which represents the amount of light reflected from an unpolished surface in proportion to the total amount of light falling upon it. The albedo of the Moon and Mercury is 7; of Venus, 59; of the Earth, 44; of Mars, 15.

ALBUMAZAR
An Asiatic astrologer who flourished in the ninth century A.D. He was the author of many astrological treatises that exerted a great influence in the Middle Ages.

ALCHANDRUS
Ancient astrologer. There is extant a work of his dealing with

the motions of the planets, the zodiacal signs, and in general the principles of astrology.

ALCUIN
English scholar who belongs in the eighth century. He was the educational and cultural adviser to the Emperor Charlemagne. Alcuin was said to have been deeply interested in astrological studies.

ALEXANDER IN INDIA
It was said that when Alexander the Great advanced into India he was instructed by an Indian ruler in the esoteric principles and techniques of astrology.

ALFONSO X
(1221-1284) Alfonso X of Castile, called the Wise, regarded astrology as one of the liberal sciences: that is, one of the seven disciplines called the Liberal Arts in the Middle Ages. He granted astrologers the right to practice their art, and added that the predictions made by astrology were to be observed in the natural course or motions of the planets.

AL KINDI, JACOB
Arab scientist and philosopher who belongs in the ninth century A.D. He was a mathematician, astronomer, and astrologer, and taught at the school of astrology in Bagdad. Author of *De judiciis astrorum*, The Judgments of the Stars.

ALMANAC
A book or table containing a calendar of days, weeks, and months, to which are added astronomical or other data. Its use dates back to which are added astronomical or other data. One almanac now in the British Museum dates from the time of Rameses II (1292-1225 B.C.). The Alexandrian Greeks also used almanacs. The *fasti* — days on which business could be transacted — were listed in the Roman almanac. The earliest almanac of which we have any precise record is that of Solomon Jarchus, 1150 A.D. Purbach published an almanac from 1450-1456. His

pupil Regiomontanus issued the first printed almanac in 1475. The most outstanding almanac maker of the Middle Ages was Nostradamus. All English almanacs were prophetic until the year 1824, and until 1834 the stamp duty was IIs. 3 d. per copy. The first almanac in the United States was issued in 1639 by William Pierce. It was exceeded in popularity by *Poor Richard's Almanack* (1732-1757) issued by Benjamin Franklin. *Watkins' Almanack,* issued since 1868, has an annual circulation of more than two million copies. The chief Astrological Almanacs of the present period are *Raphael's* first published in 1820; and *Zadkiel's* first published in 1830.

AL MISRI
Architect who belongs in the ninth century A.D. Wrote a commentary on Ptolemy's *Tetrabiblos*: also the author of a number of astrological works, including a manual on the subject.

ALTITUDE
This is the elevation above the horizon, measured by the arc of a vertical circle. A planet is at meridian altitude when it is at the Midheaven, the cusp of the Tenth House.

AMERICAN FEDERATION OF ASTROLOGERS
This is an organization whose members are or become professional astrologers. It grants certificates to competent students.

ANARETA
This term, which is of Greek origin, means *destroyer*. In astrology, it is the planet that kills, for it applies to a planet that unfavorably aspects the hyleg.

ANATOMICAL SIGNS
In astrology, the signs are associated with different parts of the human anatomy, as follows:
Aries: head
Taurus: neck
Gemini: arms

Cancer: chest
Leo: back and heart
Virgo: abdomen
Libra: loins, kidney
Scorpio: organs of generation
Sagittarius: thighs
Capricorn: knees
Aquarius: legs
Pisces: feet

ANAXAGORAS
Greek philosopher of the fifth century B.C. He was reputed to be skilled in astrology.

ANAXIMANDER
Greek philosopher of the sixth century B.C. He was reputed to be an astrologer.

ANCIENT ASTROLOGY
In Iranian mythology, the supreme benefic spirit, Ahura Mazda, was equated astrologically with the deity who ruled the heavens. In antiquity, astrology was interested in the putative influence of the heavenly bodies on the destinies of men. It also asserted that astrology could predict occurrences on earth as dependent on the planets. Mesopotamia elaborated these concepts which later on spread to Egypt.

ANCIENT DOCTRINE
In antiquity there was an astrological concept that the moon governs the physical life and that the sun is the source of the intellectual life and governs the reasoning faculty.

ANCIENT INTEREST
In antiquity, astrology was studiously cultivated by the Jewish philosophers. Sir Christopher Heydon, who belongs in the seventeenth century and who wrote a Defense of Judicial Astrology, declared that Moses himself, an adept in many occult fields, was proficient in astrologers' techniques.

ANCIENT RECORDS
In antiquity, in the Near East, observations were made by the star-gazers and recorded on tablets. These observations were interpreted in an occult sense. The accumulated comments and records have constituted the basis and sources of astrological knowledge for the last five thousand years.

AN EVENING'S LOVE
A play by the English dramatist and poet John Dryden (1631-1700), in which a pseudo-astrologer appears.

ANGELIC ASTROLOGERS
In the nineteenth century, when astrological studies were experiencing a popular renaissance, many editors of astrological periodicals and also writers of astrological texts adopted seraphic names such as Zadkiel, Raphael, Sepharial.

ANGELIC ASTROLOGY
Certain planets are astrologically associated with angels. For example: Sun, with Michael. Moon, with Gabriel. Mercury, with Raphael. Venus, with Arnad. Mars, with Samael. Jupiter, with Zadkiel. Saturn, with Cassiel. Uranus, with Arvath.

ANGELS
Astrologically, the angel Samael is associated with Mars: Cassiel with Saturn: Anael with Venus: Zadkiel with Jupiter.

ANGLE
Any of the four cardinal points in a Figure, or map, of the heavens; variously referring to the Zenith, or South Vertical, the Nadir, or North Vertical, and the East and West horizons: the cusps of the Tenth, Fourth, First, and Second Houses, or the Medium Coeli, Imum Coeli, Oriens (Ascendant) and Occidens (Descendant) of a Solar or of any Celestial Figure.

ANGULAR
Astrologically, the reference is to a planet in an angle or in an angular House.

ANGULAR VELOCITY
Astrologically, this is the angle through which a planet sweeps in a unit of time. Technically, the daily motion of a planet, expressed in degrees and minutes of arc, is its Angular Velocity.

ANIMAL LIFE
Aristotle's *History of Animals* discusses stellar influences on the life of animals.

ANIMALS
Not only human beings are regarded as being conditioned, throughout their lives, by the celestial system, but animals as well. In essence, it is conceived that there is astrological sympathy between the cosmic phenomena and all phenomena associated with the earth.

ANNUS MAGNUS
A Latin expression meaning *The Great Year*. Astrologically, it denotes the first year of the universe. According to some Romans, among them Pliny the Elder and the poet-astrologer Manilius, the Annus Magnus began at noon when the Spring Equinox occurred among the stars of Aries.

ANOMALY
Astrologically, the angular distance of a planet from its perihelion or aphelion.

ANTIPATHIES
Astrologically, the unaccountable aversions and antagonisms that people feel toward each other when positions in their Nativities are in conflict.

ANTIPATHY
Astrologically, the disharmony of two bodies, usually planets, which rule or are exalted in opposite Signs. For example, Saturn ruling Capricorn has an antipathy for the Moon ruling Cancer.

ANTIQUITY OF ASTROLOGY
In Hindu traditions, the ancient astrologer Asuramaya, who was reputed to have been born in Atlantis, confirmed the high antiquity of the art itself.

ANTISCION
In Iranian astrology, this term denotes the reflex position of a planet's birth position, in that degree on the opposite side of the Cancer-Capricorn axis, of which either no degrees Cancer or no degrees Capricorn is the midpoint.

ANTISEDENTIA
Astrologically, this is an older term describing retrograde motion.

APHETA
In astrology, this is the prorogator. The planet or place that exercises an influence over the life and death of the native.

APHOREL
A British astrologer whose real name was F. W. Lacey. Several astrologers have used as their professional signatures seraphic names: such as Zadkiel and Sepharial. Aphorel belongs in the early twentieth century. He was co-publisher of *The Astrologer's Magazine.*

APHORISM
Astrologically, this term refers to considerations involved in the summing-up or synthesis of the various testimonies in the Figure.

APOCALYPSE
The Apocalypse contains a great deal of matter relating to astrological concepts and symbolism.

APOGEE OF ASTROLOGY
Astrology reached its height in the sixteenth century, with every prince and ruler attended by his own personal astrologer. Cathe-

rine de Médici had two astrologers: Cosmo Ruggieri and Ogier Ferrier.

APPLICATION
Astrologically, this term refers to a body in motion toward a point whence it will aspect another body.

APPULSE
Astrologically, the appulse is the approach of one orbital body toward another.

APSIS
Astrologically, the points of greatest and least distance of a heavenly body from its centre of attraction.

APULEIUS
Roman philosopher and novelist who flourished in the second century A.D. His works are interspersed with discussions and references relating to occult practices and magic. Astrological treatises too have been attributed to his authorship.

AQUARIUS
In astrology, the Water-carrier. The eleventh, southern sign of the zodiac. Mystically, Aquarius is associated with the Great Flood. Kabalistically, this sign stands for the legs of the archetypal man and the locomotive functions of the human organism.

ARAB CONCEPT
To the ancient Arab astrologers, all variations and changes that took place in the terrestrial sphere were connected with the movement of the celestial bodies.

ARAB CULTURE
The rulers of Arabia were for the most part patrons of education and culture. They spent vast monies in accumulating libraries and in sending research scholars throughout all parts of the world. They erected observatories, developed optics, and com-

piled catalogues of the stars. The stories in the *Thousand And One Nights* abound in references to astrology and astromancy. Al-Mamun, the son of the famous Al-Raschid, ordered the astronomical and astrological books of Ptolemy to be translated into Arabic. It is also now conceded that this Caliph was himself versed in astrology and that he frequently employed it in administering the state.

ARAB SOURCES
The astrology of the Arabs is believed to have drawn material from Greek sources, from Ptolemy, and from Egyptian and Mesopotamian traditions.

ARABIAN POINTS
Also known as Arabian Parts. Astrologically, Fortuna, or the Part of Fortune, is best known. Instead of revolving the Figure, the Arabs gave rules whereby planetary House positions could be inserted in a Figure based on a birth-moment.

ARABIC TRANSLATION
The oldest rendering of Ptolemy's *Tetrabiblos* was made in Arabic by Ishaq ben Hunein, in the ninth century A.D.

ARAB INTEREST
The Arabs were so interested in astrology that in 827 A.D. Ptolemy's *Megale Syntaxis* was translated into Arabic under the title of *Almagest*.

ARC
Astrologically, a portion or segment of a curved line, such as a circle or ellipse. Hence the orbital distance separating two bodies, or between two points.

ARCHITECTURE AND ASTROLOGY
Vitruvius the Roman author of a treatise on architecture belongs in the first century A.D. He relates architectural plans and calculations to astrological techniques. He also makes other references

to astrological principles and to the Chaldeans as adepts in astrological computations.

ARC OF VISION
In astrology, the least distance from the Sun at which a planet is visible when the Sun is below the horizon.

ARIES
The Ram. The first, northern sign of the zodiac. In Egyptian religion, the deity Amon-Ra was represented with ram's horns.

ARISTOTLE ON STARS
Aristotle regarded the stars as beings of superhuman intelligence, incorporate deities.

ARMILLARY SPHERE
In astrology, a skeleton sphere suggested by concentric rings of the celestial circles of the equator and the ecliptic revolving within a horizon and meridian divided into degrees of longitude and latitude. It was invented by Eratosthenes who by this means computed the size of the earth, and inclination of the ecliptic to the equator; also the latitude of the city of Alexandria. The armillary sphere is often used as a decoration. There is a specimen cast in bronze and supported on the shoulders of Atlas, at Rockefeller Plaza, New York.

ARTAXERXES
Ancient king of Persia, who had at his court, as physician and astrologer, the Greek Scholar, physician, and historian Ctesias, who belongs in the late fifth century B.C.

ASCENDANT
Astrologically, the ascendant is the rising degree of the ecliptic.

ASCENDING
Astrologically, this term refers to any planet on the eastward side of the line between the cusps of the Fourth and Tenth

Houses, which by the diurnal motion of the Earth is rising in the heavens.

ASCENSION
Astrologically, the vertical rising of a planet above the Ecliptic, equator, or horizon.

ASCENSION, SIGNS OF LONG
Astrologically, these signs are: Cancer, Leo, Virgo, Libra, Scorpio, Sagittarius.

ASCENSION, SIGNS OF SHORT
In astrology, these signs are: Capricorn to Gemini inclusive.

ASCENSIONAL DIFFERENCE
Astrologically, the difference between the Right Ascension of any body and its Oblique Ascension.

ASHMOLE, ELIAS
(1617 - 1692) English antiquarian and occultist. Interested in alchemy. Versed in branches of astrology. Friend of many contemporary astrologers, among them Richard Saunders and William Lilly, author of *Introduction to Astrology*.
In his collection of alchemical and astrological lore entitled *Theatrum Chemicum Britannicum*, Ashmole declared that astrology is a profound science.

ASPECTS
Astrologically, the aspects of the planets in relation to each other. These aspects determine the significance, whether favorable or not, of the planet. The more important aspects are:
Trine, marked △ when two planets are four signs apart.
Sextile, marked * when two planets are two signs apart.
Quintile, when two planets are 72° apart.
These three aspects are favorable.
Conjunction σ when two planets or stars are of the same sign.

This aspect may be favorable or unfavorable.
Opposition ∞ when two planets are six signs apart.
Quartile ☐ when two planets are three signs apart.
Semi-quartile ½ ☐ when two planets are 45° apart.
These last three aspects are unfavorable.

ASSYRIA
In ancient Assyria there were cuneiform tablets, composed of clay, in the library of Ashurbanipal, that dealt with astrological issues.

ASTERISM
Astrologically, a constellation. Sometimes misleadingly applied to a zodiacal sign. But asterism may be applied to the three signs of the same element.

ASTEROIDS
Astrologically, the asteroids Ceres, Juno, Pallas, Vesta are of dubious influence.

ASTRO-BIOLOGY
A term in use by German astrologers. They have investigated the psychological aspects of the individual in relation to astrological influences upon the total individual.

ASTROLATRY
This term denotes the worship of the stars. In antiquity, particularly in the Middle East, among the Chaldeans, astrolatry was a regular practice.

ASTROLOGERS INTERNATIONAL, LTD.
A current organization devoted to astrological techniques and issues.

ASTROLOGERS' INVOCATION
Firmicus Maternus, who belongs in the fourth century A.D. and

wrote an astrological treatise entitled *Mathesis,* introduces his theme with reverence:

But lest my words be bereft of divine aid and the envy of some hateful man impugn them by hostile attacks, whoever thou art, God, who continuest day after day the course of the heavens in rapid rotation, who dost perpetuate the mobile agitation of ocean's tides, who dost strengthen earth's solidity in the immovable strength of its foundation, who dost refresh with night's sleep the toil of our earthly bodies, who when our strength is renewed dost return the grace of sweetest light, who dost stir all the substance of thy work by the salutary breath of the winds, who dost pour forth the waves of streams and fountains in tireless force, who dost revolve the varied seasons by sure periods of days: sole governor and prince of all, sole emperor and lord, whom all the celestial forces serve, whose will is the substance of perfect work, by whose faultless laws all nature is forever adorned and regulated; thou father alike and mother of everything, thou bound to thyself, father and son, by one bond of relationship; to thee we extend suppliant hands, thee with trembling supplication we venerate; grant us grace to attempt the explanation of the courses of thy stars; thine is the power that somehow compels us to that interpretation. With a mind pure and separated from all earthly thoughts and purged from every stain of sin we have written these books for thy Romans.

ASTROLOGERS' SOCIETY

There was an Astrologer's Society in London in the seventeenth century. Elias Ashmole, the antiquary and astrologer, was associated with the Society.

ASTROLOGER TO CARDINAL

James Gaffarel was the official astrologer to the famous French statesman Cardinal Richelieu (1585-1642).

ASTROLOGICAL AGES

Anciently, a period of some 2,000 years, during which the Point of the Spring Equinox recedes through one sign of the Zodiac of Constellations. Since the constellations have no precise boundaries, the points of beginning and ending are mere approximations. It is absurd, however, to date the beginning of the precessional cycle, of presumably 25,000 years, from the particular time in history when it was decided no longer to treat the Equinox as a moving point, but instead to freeze it at no degrees Aries. It is probable that midway between the Equinoctial points are the Earth's Nodes, where the plane of its orbit intersects that of the Sun, at an inclination of approximately 50 degrees. But since the Equinoctial point is now considered as a fixed point and the motion takes place only within its frame of reference, it appears that a study of the circle which the celestial pole describes around the pole of the Ecliptic will be required in order to determine when it passes an East point, to mark the time of beginning of the first of twelve astrological ages of 2,150 years each, into which the precessional cycle is subdivided. On this manner of reckoning, the Earth might now be in the Capricorn Age as well as any other. Historical records show the Equinox as having once begun in Taurus, at which time Taurus was regarded as the first sign of the Zodiac.

ASTROLOGICAL ANALOGIES
Authorities have referred to the analogies, in an astrological sense, between the ancient Aztecs of Mexico, the Chaldeans, the Egyptians, and the Greeks.

ASTROLOGICAL ANATOMY
Astrologically, the Sun operates through the anterior pituitary gland. The Moon is the substance of the body. Mercury is associated with the thyroid gland. Venus, with the thymus gland. Jupiter, with the posterior pituitary gland. Saturn affects the medullary portion of the adrenal gland. Uranus, the parathyroid gland. Neptune, the pineal gland. Pluto, the pancreas.

ASTROLOGICAL ANECDOTE
An old woman, ignorant of the difference between astronomy

17

and astrology, once came to Greenwich Observatory to recover a bundle of linen that she had lost. John Flamstead, the first astronomer royal of England and founder of Greenwich Observatory in 1676, set up a horary chart and the linen was found in the place indicated by him.

ASTROLOGICAL BASIS
Some authorities postulated that among the early Babylonians religion was founded on astrological knowledge.

ASTROLOGICAL BOOK OF FATE
Among the ancient Aztecs, there was a Book of Good and Bad Days. To these days were attributed either beneficent or malefic conditions. Among the Romans similarly certain days were *dies fasti*, lawful days, and others were *dies nefasti*, unlawful days, when all public business was suspended and courts were closed because all such days betokened ominous occurrences.

ASTROLOGICAL CATALOGUE
In 1898 three European scholars, F. Cumont, W. Kroll, and F. Boll, with the collaboration of others, published a Catalogue of Greek astrological codices.

ASTROLOGICAL COLORS
Astrologically, the colors of the spectrum are associated with specific planets:
The Sun — orange, gold, yellow.
The Moon — white, Pearl, opal, iridescent hues.
Mercury — slate color.
Venus — sky blue, pale green.
Mars — red, carmine.
Jupiter — purple, deep blue.
Uranus — streaked mixtures.
Neptune — lavender, sea-green.
Pluto — luminous pigments.

ASTROLOGICAL CONCEPT
It was anciently postulated that the moon presides over the physical life of man, and that the sun is associated with the intellectual and rational aspect.

ASTROLOGICAL CONFERENCE
The first astrological Congress was organized in Munich, in 1923. Another congress, the following year, took place in Leipzig. Since then there have been quite a number of such symposia, both in Europe and in the USA.

ASTROLOGICAL CURES
The ancient Aztecs assigned the twenty letters or figures of their cycle, which they employed in all their calculations, to the various parts of the human body, and they cured by a knowledge of the astrological virtues of the signs those who became ill or suffered pain in the various members.

ASTROLOGICAL DAYS
Certain planets are considered to have added strength or to exercise rulership, on certain days of the week.

ASTROLOGICAL EPITAPH
John Dryden (1631-1700,) the famous English poet, wrote the following lines as an epitaph for a young Englishwoman:
For sure the milder planets did combine
On thy auspicious horoscope to shine,
And the most malicious were in trine.

ASTROLOGICAL FLAVORS
The planets are associated with certain flavors:
The Sun — sweet, pungent.
The Moon — odorless.
Mercury — astringent.
Venus — warm, sweet.
Mars — astringent, pungent.
Jupiter — fragrant.

Saturn — cold, sour.
Uranus — cold, astringent.
Neptune — seductive.
Pluto — aromatic.

ASTROLOGICAL FORMS
Certain shapes and forms are associated with specific planets:
The Sun — circles, curves.
The Moon — crooked lines.
Mercury — short lines.
Venus — curves.
Mars — angles, straight lines.
Jupiter — curves.
Saturn — short lines.
Uranus — broken lines.
Neptune — curves.
Pluto — straight lines, sharp angles.

ASTROLOGICAL JEWELS
Certain planets are associated with particular jewels and precious stones:
Sun — diamond, ruby, carbuncle.
Moon — pearl, opal, moonstone.
Mercury — quicksilver.
Venus — emerald.
Mars — bloodstone, flint.
Jupiter — amethyst, turquoise.
Saturn — garnet, all black stones.
Uranus — chalcedony, lapis lazuli.
Neptune — coral, ivory.
Pluto — beryl, jade.

ASTROLOGICAL KNOWLEDGE
Some authorities assert that astrological knowledge in the Mesopotamian region began with its introduction by the Semitic Chaldeans.

ASTROLOGICAL MANUSCRIPTS
There are extant astrological treatises attributed to Hermes Trismegistus, Hermes the Thrice Greatest. These works deal with astrological medicine, the virtues of the zodiacal signs.

ASTROLOGICAL MEDICINE
In antiquity, physicians based their treatment of diseases and the appropriate remedial measures on astrological calculations. This practice was highly popular in the Middle Ages as well, and even in contemporary times it is not obsolete.

ASTROLOGICAL METALS
Certain planets are associated with particular metals:
Sun — gold.
Moon — silver.
Mercury — quicksilver.
Venus — copper.
Mars — iron.
Jupiter — tin.
Saturn — lead.
Uranus — radium.
Neptune — lithium, platinum.
Pluto — tungsten, plutonium.

ASTROLOGICAL PATHOLOGY
Certain ailments are associated with planetary influences:
Sun — ailments of heart and spine, fevers, spleen.
Moon — endocrine imbalance, catarrhal infections.
Mercury — nervous disorders.
Venus — blood impurities.
Mars — infectious diseases.
Jupiter — maladies resulting from surfeit.
Saturn — skin diseases, rheumatism, melancholia.
Uranus — inflammations.
Neptune — glandular imbalance.
Pluto — acidosis, arthritic conditions.

ASTROLOGICAL PROGNOSTICATION
Such prognostication is divided into two principal parts. The first and more general part refers to nations, countries, cities. The second part involves, in a genethlialogical sense, individuals.

ASTROLOGICAL TABLET
Abraham the Chaldean, it was said, bore on his breast an astrological tablet on which anyone could read his own destiny.

ASTROLOGICAL TERMINOLOGY
A great part of the astrological terminology used in modern times is derived from Arab sources, particularly in the medieval period.

ASTROLOGICAL TEXTS
There are ancient astrological texts belonging in the Mesopotamian region, that postulate that the stars are deities and that predictions involve only the king, the ruler of the state.

ASTROLOGICAL TREATISES
Apollonius of Tyana, Neoplatonic philosopher and occultist who flourished in the first century A.D., is the putative author of treatises on predicting the future by reference to the stars.

ASTROLOGICAL TYPES
Professional astrologers can determine, without extensive astrological computations, whether a native belongs to the zodiacal or the planetary type.

ASTROLOGICAL VALUES
The professional astrologer usually regards predictions based on the celestial system as a mere secondary aspect of his function. His significant work rests on delineation of the character and the potential abilities of his client, derived from astrological calculations.

ASTROLOGICAL VEGETATION
Herbs are classified according to planetary influences:
Sun: almond, celandine, juniper, rue, saffron.
Moon: chickweed, hyssop, purslain, moonwart.
Mercury: calamint, endive, horehound, marjoram, pellitory, valerian.
Venus: artichoke, foxglove, ferns, sorrel, spearmint.
Mars: aloes, capers, coriander, crowfoot, gentian, ginger, honeysuckle, peppers.
Jupiter: aniseed, balm, myrrh, wort, lime, linden, nutmeg, jessamine.
Saturn: aconite, fumitory, ivy, medlar, moss, aloes, senna.
No additions to these ancient classifications have been made with regard to Uranus, Neptune, Pluto.

ASTROLOGY AMONG THE NATIONS
In the course of the centuries astrologers have made predictions with regard to military campaigns, invasions, sudden deaths of emperors and kings, disastrous floods, famine, disease. All such occurrences were reputedly the result of planetary positions and unfavorable celestial conditions.

ASTROLOGY AND DOMESTICITY
Astrology offers advice, by consultation of the stars, of dejections and exaltations, conjunctions and oppositions, on when and whom to marry, on the propitious time for any undertaking, on favorable days for certain household operations, and on a large number of small daily domestic activities.

ASTROLOGY AND RELIGION
For centuries there has been debate on whether astrology is antagonistic to orthodox religious beliefs. Many astrologers, however, have been able to reconcile astrology in the contact of the entire cosmic system.
Religious beliefs may be consonant with astrological principles, as is evident in the case of the Chinese Taoists and the Tibetan Lamas, who find no disharmony between their religious convictions and the acceptance of astrological tenets.

23

ASTROLOGY AND THE BIBLE
It is not amiss to realize that astrology was greatly cultivated by the wisest among the ancient Israelites, even by Moses himself.

ASTROLOGY AND THE BODY
The twelve zodiacal signs exert influence on various parts of the human body. The head is the province of Aries. Capricorn governs the knees. Pisces affects the feet.

ASTROLOGY AS SCIENCE
Attempts have been made at various times to demonstrate the mathematical infallibity of astrological procedures. K. E. Krafft, the Swiss astrologer who was an adviser to Hitler, sought to validate astrology as an exact science by statistical computations.

ASTROLOGY ATTACKED
Tertullian, who belongs in the third century A.D., was a Christian theologian and a polemical writer. To Tertullian astrology was invented by the fallen angels. The practice of astrology, he insisted, should be shunned by Christians.

ASTROLOGY, ATTITUDE TO
In Catholicism, predicting the future by the position or course of the stars, with reference to natural phenomena such as drought, storms, is regarded as lawful. With reference to foreknowledge of human actions, astrology is regarded as heretical.

ASTROLOGY, BRANCHES OF
There are distinct branches of astrology: natal or genethliacal, dealing with the birth Figure.
Horary: a Figure cast for the birth-moment of an idea or an event.
Electional: choosing the propitious moment for an undertaking.
Mundane or Judicial: referring to the influence of the planets on populations or countries or cities.
Medical: application of astrology to health.

Meteorological: application of astrology to weather conditions. Agricultural: application of astrology to planting and harvesting of crops.

ASTROLOGY IN ART

Apart from elaborate and decorative astrological charts and diagrams, various aspects of astrological interest have been represented pictorially. A Chinese picture shows the Emperor Yao with a commission of scholars organizing the calendar and paying reverence to the heavenly bodies. At Merton College, Oxford University, there are carved in stone vivid zodiacal figures. Fourteenth century miniatures on a calendar depict the occupations of the months and the signs of the zodiac. There are etchings of Nostradamus absorbed in his occult prognostications. An engraving by J. Demannez depicts a scholarly astrologer, surrounded by his charts and instruments, steeped in calculations.

There is extant a Babylonian boundary stone showing Venus, the Sun, and the Moon.

A medieval engraving depicts the Moon's influence on the minds of women. Woodcuts are numerous showing the properties of the planets.

A fifteenth century allegorical picture represents Saturn and the natives who are affected by this planet. The seven planets and the signs appear again and again through the centuries, all artistically etched or carved or painted. A Roman relief of the second century A.D. shows a child's horoscope being cast. A Dutch engraving of the eighteenth century depicts Trimalchio's Banquet with the various dishes symbolizing the Zodiac.

ASTROLOGY IN EGYPT

In the nineteenth century it was a popular custom for the Egyptians to consult an astrologer before naming a child.

ASTROLOGY, INFLUENCE OF

Astrology has currently reached such a point of widespread popularity that a New York department store advertises stationery imprinted with zodiacal notes. In other directions, too, names are borrowed from the zodiac. A company, for instance, takes the name of the Gemini X-ray Chemical Corporation. Drinking glasses are decorated with the zodiacal signs. Ladies' handbags are embroidered with Virgo and Scorpio and Libra. A watch is advertised as a Zodiac Spacetronic Watch. Cocktails are named for Taurus, Capricorn, Pisces. Other signs of the zodiac appear in commerce and industry, as follows: Sagittarius Productions, Capricorn Designs, Aries Bake Shops, Taurus Press, Aries Documentaries, Libra Studios, Leo Dresses, Pisces Antiques, Virgo Fashions. In a wider sense, college students and others all over the country are probing into astrological phenomena, sorcery, witchcraft, spiritualism, mystery cults.

ASTROLOGY IN KING LEAR
In Act I Edmund expounds: When we are sick in fortune — often the surfeit of our own behavior — we make guilty of our disasters the sun, the moon, and the stars; as if we were villains by necessity, fools by heavenly compulsion, knaves, thieves and treachers by spherical predominance, drunkards, liars, and adulterers by an enforced obedience of planetary influence.

ASTROLOGY IN MEDICINE
From the time of Hippocrates, astrology was regarded as an extremely valuable aid in diagnosing diseases.

ASTROLOGY IN ROME
The first Roman Emperor, Augustus, banished astrologers from Rome, but they were recalled by later Emperors. Tiberius, Augustus' immediate successor, had a knowledge of astrology. He had studied the science under Thrasyllus, a noted astrologer of Alexandria.

ASTROLOGY IN THE ORIENT
From the third millennium B.C. on, for some 2,500 years, the Chinese studied astronomy merely in terms of astrological values.

ASTRO-MEDICAL MANUAL
In the Middle Ages, the Canon of Avicenna (980-1037), the famous Arab physician, philosopher, and occultist, was regarded as the most authoritative source book on astro-medical matters.

ASTRONOMY-ASTROLOGY
Throughout the course of Arab culture, the astronomer and the astrologer were not distinguished, as the knowledge of one was absorbed equally by the other's knowledge.

ASTROTHEOLOGY
A system of theology founded on what is known of the heavenly bodies and of the laws which regulate their movements.

ASURAMAYA
Ancient Hindu magician and astrologer. He was reputed to have been born, according to occult tradition, in Atlantis.

ATEN
In astrology, this is the solar disc or the light that proceeds from the sun.

ATHAZER
Astrologically, an ancient term applied to the Moon when in conjunction with the Sun or separated from it by an arc of twelve degrees, forty-five degrees, ninety degrees, one hundred-fifty degrees, one hundred-sixty degrees, one hundred-eighty degrees.

AUGUSTINUS, AURELIUS
(354-430) St. Augustine, the eminent Church Father, discussed and examined the values of certain disciplines inherited from antiquity. He estimated these disciplines in relation to their contribution to the spiritual life. With regard to astrology, he was consistently hostile to its practice.

AUGUSTUS
C. Octavius Augustus, the first Roman emperor (63 B.C.-14 A.D.) was interested in astrology. He had a silver coin minted on which Capricorn, his birth sign, was stamped.

AVENAR
A Jewish astrologer who flourished in the fifteenth century. He computed the advent of a Hebraic Messiah.

AXIAL ROTATION
The diurnal motion of the Earth around its axis; or a similar motion by any other celestial body.

AXIS, INCLINATION OF
There is an inclination of the axis in relation to the plane of the orbit.

AZIMENE
This term refers to a planet posited in certain or lame degrees or arcs which, if ascending at birth, were regarded as making the native blind or lame, or otherwise afflicted.

AZIMUTH
A point of the horizon and a circle extending to it from the zenith; or an arc of the horizon measured clockwise between the south-point of the horizon and a vertical circle passing through the centre of any object.

AZTEC FORECASTS
Like the Egyptians, the Greeks, and the Romans, the augurs among the Mexican Aztecs foretold events from the positions of the planets, the arrangements of sacred numbers, from clouds, storms, eclipses, comets, the flight of birds and the actions of animals.

AZTEC PREDICTIONS
The Aztecs of ancient Mexico were deeply involved in astrol-

ogical practices. In the early years of the sixteenth century an eclipse occurred which according to those proficient in interpreting the stars, betokened disaster. The disaster was a tremendous earthquake.

AZTECS

On the birth of a child, the Aztecs instantly summoned an astrologer. His duty was to ascertain the destiny of the newborn infant.

AZTEC SIGNS

The twenty signs of the Zodiac with their Aztec names and English equivalents are as follows:

1.	Cipactli	The Crocodile
2.	Eecatl	The Wind
3.	Calli	The House
4.	Cuelzpalin	The Lizard
5.	Couatl	The Snake
6.	Miquiztli	Death
7.	Macatl	The Deer
8.	Tochtli	The Rabbit
9.	Atl	The Water
10.	Itzcuintli	The Dog
11.	Ocamatli	The Ape
12.	Malinalli	The Twisted
13.	Acatl	The Reed
14.	Ocelotl	The Jaguar
15.	Quauhtli	The Vulture
16.	Cozcaquauhili	The Eagle
17.	Olin	Motion (the Sun)
18.	Tecpatl	The Flint Knife
19.	Quiauitl	The Rain
20.	Xochitl	The Flower

AZTEC TONALAMATH

Tonalamath is the title of an ancient Aztec calendar in which auspicious or malefic phenomena are associated with certain days.

BABYLONIA
In Babylonia, which is regarded as the fountainhead of astrological studies, astrology and astronomy were conjoined. In the Middle Ages, also, one of the four disciplines of the quadrivium was astrology combined with astronomy.
Although astrological studies had their source in Babylonia, China too had an ancient astrological tradition. Similarly with the Aztecs, the Mayans, and the Incas.

BABYLONIAN ASTROLOGERS
The astrologers of ancient Babylon, asserted an authority, regarded astronomy only as an aid in computing the positions of the stars.

BABYLONIAN DEITIES
Among the Babylonians the deities were associated with some particular planet: the god Marduk was attached to Jupiter. Sin was related to the Moon. Ishtar was related to Venus. Nergal was linked with Mars.

BACON, FRANCIS

(1561-1626) Elizabethan statesman and scholar. He had an inclination toward astrological belief and did not consider that it should be totally rejected. With regard to relation of astrology and prophecy, he states: Predictions may be made of comets to come, which (I am inclined to think) may be foretold; of all kinds of meteors, of floods, droughts, heats, frosts, earthquakes, eruptions of water, eruptions of fire, great winds and rains, various seasons of the year, plagues, epidemic diseases, plenty and dearth of grain, wars, sedition, schisms, transmigrations of people and any other or all commotions or general revolutions of things, natural as well as civil.

BANDS AROUND JUPITER

The bands or zones that encircle the planet Jupiter are known as the Belts of Jupiter.

BARREN SIGNS

These signs are: Gemini, Leo, Virgo. The Moon in Sagittarius and Aquarius is also said to signify a tendency toward barrenness.

BAYLE, PIERRE

(1647-1706) French philosopher who attacked the validity of astrology as an exact science.

BEDE

The Venerable Bede, who belongs in the eighth century, was a theologian and a historian. He was said to have shown deep interest in astrological studies.

BEDFORD HOURS

A fifteenth century painting that depicts the progression of the seasons and the zodiacal signs. Now in the British Museum.

BEHOLDING SIGNS
These are the signs which have the same declination, that is, which are at equal distance from the Tropics, as Aries and Virgo, Taurus and Leo, Gemini and Cancer, Libra and Pisces, Scorpio and Aquarius, Sagittarius and Capricorn. Because such pairs of signs were either both Northern, or both Southern, they were regarded by Ptolemy as of 'equal power.' This consideration, however, applied only when two such signs were joined by a body in each, mutually configurated.

BELEPHANTES
According to the Greek historian Diodorus Siculus, Belephantes was a Chaldean astrologer. He rightly predicted that Alexander the Great's entry into Babylon would be fatal to the Emperor.

BELTS OF JUPITER
A varying number of dusky belt-like bands or zones encircling the planet Jupiter, parallel to its equator. It suggests the existence of an atmosphere, the clouds forced into a series of parallels through the rapidity of rotation, the dark body of the planet showing through relatively clear spaces between.

BENEFIC ASPECTS
The planetary relations or familiarities which permit the unobstructed release of cosmic energy. The so-called benefics are: Venus, Jupiter, and possibly the Sun.

BENEVOLENT GODS
There was a traditional belief among the ancient Egyptians that, in their benevolent indulgence, the gods bestowed the gift of astrology on mankind.

BEROSUS
A Babylonian priest of Bel, who belongs in the third century B.C. He is the author of a history of Babylon from the origins to the death of Alexander the Great. He also established a college for the study of astrology, on the Greek island of Cos,

in 280 B.C. Many manuals relating to witchcraft and magic were attributed to his authorship.

BESIEGED
A benefic planet situated between two malefics, within orbs of each, is said to be besieged and therefore unfortunately placed. Some astrologers restrict the application of the term to a Significator when between and within orbs of two benefics. In earlier times, the expression referred to a planet situated between any two planets. It was then considered that a planet between Venus and Jupiter was favorably besieged. But if the planet was between Mars and Saturn it was in an extremely unfavorable position.

BESTIAL SIGNS
These are the signs which have been symbolized by animals: Aries, Taurus, Scorpio, part of Sagittarius, Capricorn, Pisces.

BICORPOREAL
This term refers to double-bodied zodiacal signs: Gemini, Sagittarius, Pisces. Ptolemy denoted by this term the mutable or deductive signs. To Ptolemy, Virgo also was bicorporeal.

BIRTH MOMENT
What is generally accepted as the true moment of birth is the moment of the first inspiration of breath after ligation of the umbilical cord. At that moment the infant ceases to receive blood conditioned through the mother's receptivities, and in response to the law of adaptability must grow channels of receptivity to cosmic frequencies that accord with those present in the Earth's magnetic field, and through these receptivities it begins to condition its own blood. This moment must be reduced to Standard Time, adjusted to Greenwich world-time for calculating the planet's places, thence readjusted to Local Mean Time at the birth place to determine the Ascendant and the Midheaven degrees and the House-cusps.

Albrecht Dürer's woodcut of the skies of the northern hemisphere, 1515.

Tycho Brahe in his observatory at Hven.

BIRTH OF ALEXANDER
At the birth of Alexander the Great Nectanebus, a magician and occultist, predicted that the new-born infant would be ruler over the entire world.

BITTER SIGNS
This expression refers to the Fire Signs: Aries, Leo, Sagittarius. They were regarded as hot, fiery and bitter.

BOLINGBROKE, ROGER
Bolingbroke was an English wizard who flourished in the fifteenth century. He was notoriously reputed to be a necromancer, adept also in astrology and the Black Arts. In the reign of King Henry VI of England he was hanged for using witchcraft in an attempt to kill the monarch.

BOLOGNA
It is said there was a chair in astrology at the University of Bologna early in the twelfth century.

BON
The priestly Bon initiates of Tibet are credited with being the sole repositories of the complicated astrological system that ensures accurate predictions.

BONATTI, GUIDO
An Italian astrologer and adept in the Black Arts, who flourished in the thirteenth century. He wrote prolifically on these subjects. He was reputed to have made an apothecary wealthy by fashioning a wax figure of a ship and endowing it with magic properties.
Like Michael Scot the occultist, he was consigned to Hell by Dante.

BRAHE, TYCHO
(1546-1601) Famous Danish astronomer who formulated many important observations, discovered a new star, and perfected astronomical instruments. On the island of Ven he built the

Castle of Uranienborg and also the observatory named Stjarneborg. Tycho Brahe also acted as astronomer and almanac maker to the family of Frederick II of Denmark.

BRAHE'S PREDICTION
Tycho Brahe, the famous astronomer, once made a remarkable prediction. From a study of the great comet of 1577 he declared that in the North, in Finland, there would be born a prince who would lay waste Germany and then vanish in 1632.
Prince Gustavus Adolphus was born in Finland. He ravaged Germany during the Thirty Years' War, and died in 1632.

BRAHMANASPATI
In Hindu astrology, this term denotes the planet Jupiter. In Vedic mythology, it is known as Brihaspati, signifying the power of prayer.

BROUGHTON, LUKE
(1824-1899) Noted American physician and astrologer who published an astrological journal called *Broughton's Monthly Planet Reader*.

BROWNING
Robert Browning's poem on Ben Ezra refers to Abraham ibn Ezra, a twelfth century Jewish philosopher and astrologer. Author of *De Nativitalibus*, Nativities.

BRUHESEN, PETER VAN
A Dutch physician and astrologer. He flourished in the sixteenth century. Author of an astrological almanac.

BUDDHISTS
Buddhists postulate the planetary influences on the terrestrial sphere and on mankind.

BUTLER'S DEFENSE
Dr. Joseph Butler, a theologian who belongs in the seventeenth century, violently attacked the principles and practice of as-

trology. In order to confirm his views, he studied astrological treatises. In the event, he became a warm partisan and defender of the art. He published his defense in 1680.

BYRON, GEORGE

(1788-1824) English poet. In his play *Sardanapalus* the theme involves astrology and one of the leading characters is the treacherous astrologer Beleses.

Byron himself was interested in astrology: he cast his son's horoscope.

BYZANTINE ASTROLOGER

Leo VI called Leo the Philosopher, was Byzantine Emperor from 886-911 A.D. He was versed in occultism and also practiced astrology.

BYZANTIUM

During the early Christian centuries Byzantium flourished in astrological studies. The Byzantine Emperors had their own official prognosticators who helped to determine imperial policies.

CADENT
Cadent houses are those which fall away from the angles: the third, sixth, ninth, and twelfth houses. Cadent planets are those which occupy cadent houses and whose influence is thereby weakened.

CAESAR
In addition to his statesmanship and his military command, Julius Caesar was also interested in astronomy-astrology. He wrote a treatise entitled *De Astris*, The Stars.

CALCULATIONS OF THE CUSPS
The best known systems for calculating the cusps of the intermediate Houses are as follows:

Campanus: The vertical circle from the Zenith to the east and west points of the horizon is trisected. Through these points are drawn the House circles, from the north and south points of the horizon. The house cusps are the points at which the ecliptic at that moment intersects the horizon.

Regiomontanus: The celestial circle is trisected, instead of the prime vertical, and great circles extend from north and south points of the horizon to the points of trisection. The house cusps are at the points at which the ecliptic intersects the horizon. At the equator the two systems give the same cusps, the disparity increasing as one approaches the earth's poles.

Horinzontal: Starting with great circles at the meridian and ante-meridian, the horizon and the prime vertical, add other great circles from zenith to nadir which trisect each quadrant of the horizon. The cusps will then be the points at which on a given moment the ecliptic intersects the vertical circles.

Placidus: The diurnal motion of the earth causes a celestial object to intersect the cusp of the twelfth House, after a sidereal-time interval equal to one-third of its semi-diurnal arc: to intersect the cusp of the eleventh House after a sidereal-time interval equal to two-thirds of its semi-diurnal arc; and to culminate at the meridian after an interval of sidereal time that corresponds to the semi-diurnal arc. The semi-arc from the meridian that intersects the eastern horizon gives the Ascendant; and the second and third House cusps are similarly extended below the horizon. The Placidian cusps are now in almost universal use.

CALENDAR

A system of reckoning and recording the time when events occur. Time is reckoned by the Earth's rotation on its axis with reference to the Sun, a day: by the Moon's revolution around the Earth, a month: by the Earth's revolution around the Sun, a year.

The Mohammedan calendar is strictly a lunar calendar, the year consisting of twelve lunar months. The Egyptian calendar divided the year into twelve months of thirty days each, with five supplementary days following each twelfth month.

The Hindu calendar is one of the early lunisolar calendars. The year is divided into twelve months, with an intercalated month bearing the same name, inserted after every month in which there are two lunations, which is about every three years.

The Chinese calendar begins with the first new moon after the Sun enters Aquarius. It consists of twelve months, with an intercalary month every thirty months, each month being divided into thirds.

The Jewish calendar is a lunisolar calendar, which reckons from 3761 B.C., the traditional year of the Creation.

In Anglo-Saxon the year began on December 25th, until William the Conqueror ordered it to begin on January Ist, the day of his coronation.

CALVIN, JOHN
(1509-1564) The celebrated theologian and reformer condemned the practice of astrological investigations.

CAMPANELLA, TOMMASO
(1568-1639) Italian philosopher: Dominican monk. Practiced astrology combined with magic in behalf of Pope Urban VIII. Author of *Astrologia*, published in 1629.

CANCER
Astrologically, the Crab. The fourth, northern sign of the zodiac. In the mystery cult of Orpheus, it is the entrance of the soul into incarnation. In occultism, this sign stands for tenacity to life. Kabalistically, it signifies the vital organs of the grand old man of the skies and therefore the life forces.

CANTERBURY TALES
Geoffrey Chaucer's *Canterbury Tales* are filled with astrological allusions: in the Physician's Tale, The Miller's, The Lawyer's, The Wife of Bath's, The Franklin's, The Knight's Tale.

CAPRICORN
Astrologically, the Goat. The tenth, southern sign of the zodiac. It represents the dual movement of life plunging into the depths and reaching toward the heights. Esoterically it is viewed as the scapegoat of the Israelites. Kabalistically, this sign stands for the knees of the grand old man of the heavens and is the emblem of material servitude.

CARDANO, GERONIMO
(1501-1576) Latinized name — Hieronymus Cardanus. An eminent Italian Kabalist, physician, mathematician, and astrologer. He is the author, among other works, of an astrological treatise in which he expounds astrological principles and techniques in terms of mathematics and he also examines the horoscopes and lives of distinguished men, in relation to their planetary influences. In another treatise, entitled *De Subtilitate*, published in 1550, he discusses demons, charms, and philtres.

CARDINAL SIGNS
These signs are: Aries, Cancer, Libra, Capricorn, whose cusps coincide with the cardinal points of the compass. Aries is East: Cancer, North: Libra, West: Capricorn, South.

CASTING NATIVITIES
Vitruvius, who belongs in the first century A.D., is the author of a treatise on architecture, in which there are passing references to astrological techniques, especially with regard to prognostication of weather conditions and casting nativities.

CATACLYSMIC PLANET
This expression refers to Uranus, which combines both the magnetic and the electric elements, producing sudden affects.

CATHERINE DE MEDICIS
(1519-1589) Queen of France. She was versed in astrology and was a patron of Nostradamus (1503-1566), the celebrated French physician and astrologer.

CATO'S WARNING
In the second century B.C. the Roman statesman, Cato the Elder, advised farmers to shun the Chaldeans. The Chaldeans, like the mathematici, were the astrologers and casters of horoscopes, the professional prognosticators.

CAZIMI
Astrologically, this Arabian term refers to the centre of the solar disc.

CECCO D'ASCOLI
A fourteenth century Italian poet and philosopher. He lectured on astrology at the University of Bologna. Previously, he had been astrologer at the court of the Duke of Florence. For his heretical views he was burned at the stake.

CELESTIAL DIVINITY
In antiquity and even in later centuries the heavenly bodies were conceived as divine beings or as divine animals.

CELESTIAL SIGN
The Roman Emperor Constantine I, called The Great (280-337), adopted Christianity as the result of a celestial phenomenon: the appearance of a cross and the expression *in hoc signo vinces*: by this sign you will conquer.

CELSUS
A Greek Platonist who belongs in the second century A.D. He was favorably disposed to astrology. He conceived the fixed stars and the planets as offering distinct prophecies.

CENSORINUS
A Roman scholar who flourished in the third century A.D. He is the author of a treatise dealing in part with the influence of the planets on human life. The work is entitled *De die natali*, The Natal Day.

CHALDEAN
The Chaldean priests and astrologers of antiquity were repeatedly banished from Rome and Italy under the first emperors.

CHAMPOLLION, JEAN FRANCQIS
Early nineteenth century French Egyptologist (1790-1832). De-

ciphered Egyptian hieroglyphics on the Rosetta Stone. In the tomb of Rameses V he discovered papyri inscribed with tables of constellations and their influences on human beings.

CHANGE IN PLANETS
In his *Tetrabiblos* Ptolemy states that the stars change to masculine or feminine. As morning stars preceding the Sun they are masculine. As evening stars following the Sun they are feminine.

CHARACTERIAL TERMINOLOGY
The association between human character and the influences of the stars and planets has penetrated into the English language. A martial individual is connected with Mars. Jovial stems from Jove or Jupiter. Mercurial describes a temperamental person and is related to Mercury. Saturnine reflects the planet Saturn.

CHARACTERISTICS OF HERBS, PLANTS, AND TREES
So much of their lives are derived from the atmosphere. Thus an herb of the Sun will often cure a malignacy caused by the Moon. Herbs of the Moon will also, under certain conditions, assist in correcting the illnesses caused by that luminary. The most common and natural means of receiving the planetary virtues of plants is from vegetables and fruits.

CHARACTERISTIC OF ZODIACAL SIGNS
Ptolemy in his Tetrabiblos calls the zodiacal signs 'commanding' when they are in the summer hemisphere. Those signs that are in the winter hemisphere he calls 'obedient.'

CHARLES V
Charles V, King of France (1337-1380) had professional astrologers attached to his court. Most European courts were surrounded by prognosticators from the fourteenth to the seventeenth century.

CHATTERTON, THOMAS
(1752-1770) English poet. Author of a poem expounding the principles of astrology.

CHAUCER, GEOFFREY
(?1340-1400) Famous English poet. In his *Canterbury Tales* the amorous Wife of Bath is said to have been born under Taurus. *The Franklin's Tale*, also, contains an astrological exposition.

CHEIRO
A well-known contemporary exponent of the divinatory arts. His actual name is Count Hamon.

CHINA
In antiquity, China was one of the leading nations in astronomical study, which meant virtually astrological procedures.

CHINESE ASTROLOGY
In Chinese astrology, Taurus is the White Tiger: Leo, the Red Bird: Scorpio, the Black Dragon: Aquarius, the Black Warrior.

CHINESE CONCEPT
The ancient Chinese concept of the composition of the cosmos was that the Earth was constituted of metal and wood.

CHINESE EMPEROR
In his travels in the thirteenth century Marco Polo found in Kanbalu that the Emperor had in his court about 5000 astrologers.

CHINESE TRADITION
The oldest Chinese tradition refers to the attributes of the five planetary empires of the world and the dynasty of starry kings that preceded human rulers.

CHINESE ZODIAC
The zodiacal signs, in Chinese astrology, were identified by the names of animals: Dog, Pig, Monkey, Horse, Rat, Ox, Tiger, Hare, Fowl, Dragon, Snake, Sheep.

CHRISTIAN FATHERS

In the early Christian centuries the practice of astrology was violently attacked by many Fathers as a pagan immorality. Particularly prominent in these fulminations was St. Augustine, who belongs in the fifth century A.D. He conceived that astrology was controlled by malefic spirits.

Illustration from Raphael's *Almanac* for 1824, later claimed as predicting the death of Louis XVIII

CHRONOCRATORS

This term denotes Markers of Time. To the ancients, the longest orbits within the solar system were of Jupiter, twelve years, and Saturn, thirty years. The conjunction of Jupiter and Saturn brought periods of great global upheaval. Jupiter and Saturn were known as the chronocrators.

CHUENI

Chinese Emperor who belongs in the third millennium B.C. He computed an ephemeris of the five planetary motions.

CHURCH OF LIGHT

This institute, located in Los Angeles, made astrological investigations to determine the functional relationships between the planets and men's specific activities.

CICERO

Although Cicero, the famous Roman orator who belongs in the first century B.C., attacked certain claims of astrology, he was deeply interested in the study, and wrote a treatise, *De Divinatione*, Divination.

CIRCLES OF POSITION

These are circles that intersect the horizon and meridian and pass through a star. The position of a star is expressed thereby: but the term is now obsolete.

CITY ASTROLOGER

In Florence, in the Middle Ages, there was an official city astrologer whose function was to study the progress of the city in relation to astrological conditions.

CITY OF KAIROUAN

This city, founded in Tunis in 670 A.D., was a cultural centre for Jewish, Greek, and Arab scholars. Here, among other disciplines that constituted the Seven Liberal Arts, astrology was eagerly pursued.

CLAUDIUS
Claudius, the Roman Emperor, was an adept in astrology and practiced divination from the entrails of animals.

CLEMENT OF ALEXANDRIA
(?150-c. 220 A.D.) Greek theologian and Church Father. To Clement, astrology is defined as the science of knowledge. He supports its practice as a contribution to religious bases.

CLIMACTERICAL CONJUNCTION
This expression refers to certain Jupiter-Saturn conjunctions.

CLIMACTERICAL PERIODS
Every seventh and ninth year in a Nativity supposedly brought about through the influence of the Moon in its position in the Radix.

CLIMACTERICAL YEARS
The astrological doctrine of climacterical years is derived from the Greek philosopher Plato's dialogue entitled The Timaeus.

COLD PLANETS
This astrological expression refers to the Moon and to Saturn.

COLLANGES, GABRIEL DE
A noted French astrologer and Kabalist who flourished in the sixteenth century.

COLLECTION OF LIGHT
When a planet is in aspect to two other bodies which are not within orbs of each other, a collection of light results through the action of the intermediary planet.

COLORS
In the age when an astrologer presumed to find in a chart the answer to every kind of question that could be propounded, he frequently undertook to tell, for example which cock would

win in a cockfight merely by indicating the color associated with the strongest planet in an Horary Figure. It also was considered an index to the coloring of a person's eyes, hair, and complexion, as well as the clothes he should wear. Thus the following color chart, adduced from Wilson;

Sun: Yellow inclined to purple.
Moon: White, or a light mixture, perhaps spotted.
Mercury: Azure to light blue.
Venus: White and purple.
Mars: Fiery red.
Jupiter: Red and green mixture.
Saturn: Black.

To the Signs these colors are attributed:
Aries: White and red.
Taurus: Red and citron mixture.
Gemini: Red and white mixture.
Cancer: Green or russet.
Leo: Golden or red.
Virgo: Black with blue spots.
Libra: Dark crimson, swarthy or black.
Scorpio: Dark brown.
Sagittarius: Olive or light green.
Capricorn: Dark brown or black.
Aquarios: Sky blue.
Pisces: Pure white and glistening.

COLUMBUS
On his voyage to America, Columbus used the ephemerides of Samuel Zacuto (1450-1510), famous Spanish-Jewish mathematician and astrologer. Zacuto is the author of a treatise on astrology.

COMBUST
This astrological term refers to the position of a planet that moves more than five degrees in the direction of the sun.

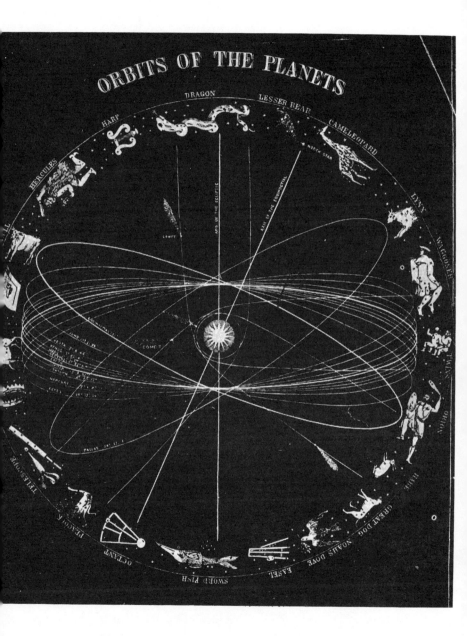

"The Orbits of the Planets Around the Sun." The major planets revolve around the sun in a narrow belt in the sky known as the Zodiac. (From Smith's *Illustrated Astronomy*, New York, 1851.)

Mosaic design from the floor of the sixth century Bet Alpha Synagogue in Israel.

COMETS
Among the Babylonians and also the Chinese, the appearance of comets was carefully noted and interpreted by the court astrologers.

COMMANDING SIGNS
These astrological signs are: Aries, Taurus, Gemini, Cancer, Leo, Virgo, because they were considered more powerful by virtue of their nearness to the zenith.

COMMON SIGNS
This astrological expression refers to the signs of the mutable quadruplicity: Gemini, Virgo, Sagittarius, Pisces. They are said to be flexible but vacillating.

CONDEMNATION
The ancient prophets of Biblical times condemned astrology and anathematized all Jews who practiced it.

On the other hand, in later centuries, the Romans were intensely interested in predictions made by astrological calculations. Cicero, in his treatise *De divinatione*, Divination, declared that no astrologer could forecast the future.

CONFIGURATION
Three or more planets in a birth map, that are joined together by aspects, whereby any stimulation will result in the combined action of all the planets which enter into the configuration.

Configuration also refers to a similar combination of mutual aspects between transitory planets.

CONFIRMATION OF SCIENTISTS
The names of many distinguished scientific minds, both ancient and modern, testify to the attraction of the astrological art. In the roster of mathematicians and astronomers and physicians who wrote on astrology or accepted its tenets may be included Hippocrates and Vitruvius, Giordano Bruno, Jerome Cardan, Copernicus and Galileo, Tycho Brahe and Regiomontanus, Roger Bacon, Flamsteed and Elias Ashmole.

CONGRESS
In 1923 a Congress of Astrologers was held in Leipzig. It may here be noted that in Germany the interest in astrology grew to tremendous and pervasive proportions from World War I on.

CONJUNCTION
Astrologically, when two planets are in the same degree of a zodiacal sign, the position is called conjunction. It may signify a favorable or unfavorable outcome.

CONQUERORS
The four greatest conquerors of historical times believed in the celestial government of the world. They were Alexander the Great, Julius Caesar, Genghis Khan, and Napoleon I.

CONSTANTINE
The Roman Emperor Constantine (c. 280-337,) had an astrologer named Valens who erected the Emperor's horoscope.

CONSTANTINUS AFRICANUS
Medieval scholar who flourished in the eleventh century. He was a prolific translator. Author, among other works, of *Pantegni,* a treatise on medicine. It contains astrological references and allusions to the Critical Days.

CONSTANTIUS
Under the Christian Roman Emperor Constantius II (317-361,) it was officially forbidden to observe the rising or setting of the sun and the stars.

CONTACT
This term is usually applied to an aspect from a directed planet to a sensitive degree created by a planet at birth. In a general sense the expression implies the energy discharge which occurs when an aspect becomes operative.

CONTEMPT FOR ASTROLOGY
In Shakespeare's *King Lear* Edmund exclaims:
   My father confounded with my mother under the dragon's

tail, and my nativity was under *ursa major;* so that it follows I am rough and lecherous. 'Sfoot! I should have been that I am the maidenliest star in the firmament twinkled on my bastardizing.

CONTRA ANTISCIONS
Astrologically, these are the same degrees of declination held by stars and planets tenanting opposite signs.

CONTRA ASTROLOGOS
This Latin expression means *An Attack against Astrologers.* It is the title of a treatise by the Italian philosopher and mystic Pico della Mirandola (1463-1494).

CONVERSE DIRECTIONS
Astrologically, these are directions that are computed opposite to the order of the zodiacal signs.

CORONATION
The coronation of Queen Elizabeth I of England (1533-1603,) was predicted by Dr. John Dee, the famous mathematician and occultist and astrologer.

CORRESPONDENCE
There is assumed to be, astrologically, a correspondence or sympathy between the human body and the twelve zodiacal signs.

CO-SIGNIFICATOR
Astrologically, this term applies to planets and signs having a wind of rotary signification. Thus Aries is a co-significator of all Ascendants, because though it is not a sign ascending it is the first sign of the zodiac, as the Ascendant is the First House in the world.

COSMIC CROSS
Astrologically, two planets in opposition, each squared by a

third planet, resulting in a T-square or T-cross. A fourth planet, opposing the third and squaring the first two, forms a Grand Cross. The T-square is a dynamic influence. The Grand Cross tends to diffusion.

COSTA BEN LUCA
An astrologer who flourished in the ninth century A.D. He wrote on occult themes. During the Middle Ages his influence was marked.

COUNCILLOR GODS
Astrologically, this expression was applied by the Chaldeans to the three bright stars in a constellation, which served to mark the position of the ruling planet of that sign, when in the sign. The expression is not in use nowadays, because of the Precession and the availability of the modern Ephemerides.

COUNTRIES AND CITIES
Not only are human beings associated astrologically with the signs of the Zodiac. Countries and cities and even days of the week have their special signs. Cancer, for instance, is New York's sign. Paris is under Virgo. London is under Gemini. Scotland is influenced by Capricorn. The USA is under Gemini. Saturday belongs to Saturn. Wednesday is Mercury's day. Sunday is the day of the Sun.

COURT ASTROLOGER
In ancient China, high prestige was attached to the court astrologer. He recorded the motions of the planets, made predictions that would affect imperial policy.

COURT INTELLIGENCER
A variant expression, used in the seventeenth and early eighteenth century, for the astrologer attached to the royal court of England. The last Court Intelligencer served the court of Queen Anne, whose reign ended in 1714.

CRACOW

In 1460 by royal decree a professorship of astrology was established at the University of Cracow, in Poland. This was the university where Copernicus (1473-1543) studied both astronomy and astrology.

CREECH, THOMAS

English classical scholar. Translated into English the astrological poem of Marcus Manilius entitled *Astronomica*. Of the zodiac, Manilius wrote:
Oblique the zodiac lies,
And signs as near, or far removed in skies,
Obliquely mount, or else directly rise.
In Cancer, so immense his round, the ray
Continues long, and slowly ends the day;
While winter's Caper in a shorter track
Soon wheels it around.

CRINAS OF MARSEILLES

An ancient Greek physician who regulated patients' diets in accordance with the motion of the stars.

CRITICAL DAYS

Astrologically, these are days which coincide with the formation, by the Moon, directional or transitory, of each successive semi-square or 45 degree aspect, to its position at birth, or at the commencement of any illness, operation, or event under Horary consideration. By noting the position of the Moon at successive crises, aspects thereto will indicate the prognosis. Favorable crises occur at the sextiles of the Moon to its radical place: but the ephemeral aspects it forms while in this position determine the manner in which the crises will pass and the eventual outcome.

CTESIAS

Ctesias of Cnidos belongs in the late fifth century B.C. He was a Greek physician and also an astrologer at the court of the Persian King Artaxerxes.

The signs of the Zodiac: from Leopold of Austria's *Astrorum Scientia*, 1489

CULMINATION
Astrologically, when a planet reaches the point of midheaven, this is called the culmination.

CULPEPER, NICHOLAS
English herbalist and astrologer who belongs in the seventeenth century. Author of *The English Enlarged,* which appeared in 1653.

CUSP
Astrologically, the imaginary line which separates a sign from adjoining signs, a House from its adjoining Houses. It is also an indeterminate arc, small in size, contiguous to the boundary-line between adjacent signs and Houses, wherein there is uncertainty regarding the planet's location at a particular moment, and ambiguity regarding the planet's influence in a borderline relationship. A birth planet is stronger when it is on the cusp then when it is in the last degrees of a House. The angular cusps are unquestionably the sharpest.

CYCLE
In the second century A.D. the astronomer-astrologer Claudius Ptolemy recommended the study of the planetary cycle as follows: We must carefully examine each of the planetary conjunctions, for it is through them that a knowledge is acquired of the mysterious forces that produce generation and decay in the universe.

CYCLES
The ancient Aztecs of Mexico regarded a period of fifty-two years as a "cycle" or a "bundle."

CYCLIC YEARS
It has been asserted that, with reference to the Greek philosopher Plato's concept of a universal cycle, there is a hint of the astrological doctrine of the Magnus Annus, The Great Year. This doctrine postulates that history begins to repeat itself when the celestial bodies return to their original positions.

DAILY CONSULTATION
The Roman Emperor Vespasian was so deeply involved in astrological practices that he consulted the stars daily, with reference to his own imperial situation.

DANIEL
The prophet Daniel was the chief of the magician-astrologers in Chaldea and Babylon. He was particularly adept in the interpretation of dreams, as is evident from the Biblical context.

DANTE
In Dante's *Inferno*, fortune-tellers are consigned to Hell, with their heads turned backward.

DARIUS
Darius (c. 558-486 B.C.) the famous Persian ruler, had attached to his court the astrologer known as Al-Hakim.

DARK MOON
Astrologically, the Dark Moon is known as the demoniac Lilith, the legendary first wife of Adam. It represents the unattainable, the forbidden, the impossible.

DAY TRIPLICITY

Astrologically, it was considered that in the daytime some planets are stronger when posited in signs of a certain element: that is, Saturn in an air-sign, the Sun in a fire-sign, Mars in a water-sign, Venus in an earth-sign.

DECAN

Astrologically, ten degrees of each zodiacal sign are dedicated to a planet which assumes influence when it passes through this ten-degree space. This ten degree space is called a decan. There are thirty-six decans at ten degrees. In these the planets, except the Sun and the Moon, alternate.

DECILE

Astrologically, an aspect formed when planets are thirty-six degrees apart. It has a slightly benefic influence.

DECLINE OF ASTROLOGY

In the eighteenth century there were so many impostors, pseudo-astrologers, itinerant quacks and adventurers lacking both knowledge and skill in astrological studies, that the practice acquired a widespread stigma.

DECUMBITURE

Astrologically, this term denotes *lying down*. A horary figure erected for the moment when a person is taken ill, wherefrom to judge the possible nature, prognosis, and duration of the illness.

DEDICATED ASTROLOGERS

Both the Roman Emperor Severus and his wife Julia were knowledgeable in astrological practices.

DEDUCTIVE TYPE

Astrologically, this expression refers to a certain quality or habit of mind that characterizes those born when the Sun was in a mutable sign: Gemini, Virgo, Sagittarius, or Pisces.

DEE, DR. JOHN
(1527-1608) English mathematician who was equally interested in the occult arts. He was imprisoned for casting horoscopes and practicing enchantments against Mary, Queen of England.

DEFENDING JUDICIAL ASTROLOGY
In 1603 Sir Christopher Heydon, who belongs in the seventeenth century, published a *Defense of Judicial Astrology*. This was a reply to a treatise condemning the art of astrology, written by a certain John Chambers. Judicial Astrology deals with the motions of the celestial bodies in relation to the terrestrial life.

DEGREE RISING
Astrologically, the degree of the zodiacal sign posted on the Ascendant, or cusp of the First House at birth, and generally considered the most important in the Nativity. The rising degree is based on the exact moment of birth, or of the event for which the Figure is cast, and the correct geographical latitude and longitude. If either factor is unknown, the Figure is usually cast for sunrise, which places the Sun's degree upon the horizon, resulting in a Solar Figure. As it is based only on the earth's apparent motion around the Sun, some astrologers term it a Heliard Figure.

DEGREES
Astrologically, the celestial globe is marked by 360 degrees and each of the twelve signs of the zodiac is consequently thirty degrees.

DEJECTION
A term used in astrology to denote the position of greatest weakness of the Sun and the Moon and other planets.

DELINEATION
(1) Applied to the generally accepted composite interpretation of specific influences, such as a planet's position in a Sign or House, an aspect between two planets, or a configuration of

Dr. John Dee, distinguished sixteenth century mathematician and astrologer.

Instrument for figuring
the geocentric system of the universe.

planets:

(2) Sometimes applied to the interpretation of the Figure as a whole, but such a summing up is more properly termed a synthesis.

DEMONIAC ASTROLOGY

This phase of astrology, practiced in antiquity, involved the

prediction of events based on observation of the stars along with the aid of demoniac forces.

DENDERAH

In the Egyptian temple at Denderah, putatively dated around the fourth millennium B.C., there were found two representations of the Zodiac: one a mural design, the other on the temple ceiling.

DEPRESSION

Astrologically, the distance of a celestial body below the horizon: its horizontal distance north.

DESCARTES, RENÉ

(1596-1650) French philosopher and scientist. In his *Discours sur la Méthode* he formally condemns the study and practice of astrology.

DESTINIES OF NATIONS

The fate of nations and of large communities is interpreted by mundane astrology. Retrospectively, practicing astrologers have analyzed such cases in regard to wars, disasters, social upheavals.

DETERMINATION OF FATE

Rabbi Hannina, an ancient Jewish scholar, declared, with reference to horary astrology:

Go to the son of Levi, and tell him that the fate of the person is not decided by the constellations of the day but by those of the hour.

DETERMINISM

The determinism of the ancient Stoics was supported by the astrology that originated in Babylonia and spread to the Greco-Roman world, and that propagated a mechanistic and fatalistic concept of the universe. Hence sidereal divination negated the very basis of religion.

DETRIMENT

Astrologically, the placement of a planet in the opposite sign from that of which it is said to be the Ruler. Frequently the term is applied to Debility by sign position, which includes the opposite sign to that which it is in its Exaltation, as well as to those of which it is Ruler.

DEXTER

Astrologically, this term is applied to an aspect which is computed backward, against the order of the signs: in which the aspected body is elevated above the aspecting body.

DIAGNOSIS

In antiquity, from the time of Hippocrates, astrology was considered as an aid in the diagnosis of sickness. This association of astrology and medicine was prevalent in medieval and later times among practicing physicians.

DICHOTOMY

Astrologically, this expression of Greek origin, meaning *cut in half*, is applied to that phase of the lunar orb, or of an inferior planet, in which only half of its disc appears illuminated, that is, the First and Third Quarters, in which the body is assuming the shape of a half-moon, and in which the Moon is said to be oriental.

DIES FASTI, NEFASTI

These Latin terms refer to days on which legal business could regularly be conducted in Rome, and days on which such business could not, without expiatory sacrifice, be conducted. These days were marked on the Roman calendar thus: F (asti), N(efasti).

DIGNITIES AND DEBILITIES
Astrologically, conditions of placement wherein a planet's influence is strengthened are called Dignities; if weakened, they are called Debilities. These are of two kinds: essential and accidental.

DIRECTIONS (Also PROGRESSIONS)
Astrologically, these expressions refer to the changing influences resulting from the various moving bodies of the solar system as they affect the individual through the sensitive points produced by the impact of planetary rays during his first year of life. There are three basic systems of calculation: Transits, Primary Directions, Secondary Progressions.

DISPOSITOR
Astrologically, this term denotes the Ruler of the Sign on the cusp of a House, who is the dispositor of a planet posited in that House. When the dispositor of any planet taken as a significator is itself disposed of by the Ruler of the Ascendant, it is considered a strongly favorable indication.

DISSOCIATE SIGNS
These are adjacent signs and signs that are five signs apart: those which bear to each other a twelfth, second, sixth, or eighth House relationship.

DISTANCE
Distance in the heavens is measured in Right Ascension or Oblique Ascension, or along the Ecliptic, the Equator, or the Prime Vertical in (1) Sidereal hours and minutes of Right Ascension along the Equator: (2) degrees and minutes of arc of Oblique Ascension along the Ecliptic, and in degrees and minutes of arc of declination above or below the Equator, or of latitude above or below the Ecliptic.
Polar Distance: The angular distance of a celestial object from

the pole: 90 degrees minus the declination.
Actual intra-solar system distances are expressed in astronomical Units: ultra-solar system distances in Light Years.

DIVINATION
Plutarch, who belongs in the second century A.D., was a Greek biographer. He discussed various aspects of divination by signs, dreams, and similar techniques.

DIVINATION AND MAGIC
In ancient Egypt there was a close association between divination and magic practices. The Egyptian magicians used incantations to secure prognosticating dreams.

DIVINATORY ASTROLOGY
According to the Greek satirist Lucian, who belongs in the second century A.D., the ancient Greeks never started any undertaking, whether domestic, personal, or otherwise, without astrological consultation.

DIVINE ASTROLOGY
In Egyptian astrological records Petosiris and Necepso, two astrologers, were regarded as godlike in their prescience. They were the subject of comment by many Greek and Roman writers, among them Ptolemy and Athenaeus, Juvenal and Pliny.

DIVINE COMEDY
In Dante's *Paradise*, Canto XXII, the poet exclaims:
    ...I saw
    The sign that follows Taurus, and was in it,
    Oh glorious stars! Oh light impregnated
    With mighty virtues, from which I acknowledge
    All of my genius whatsoe'er it be,
    With you was born, and hid himself with you
    He who is father of all mortal life.

DIVINE GIFT
The ancient Egyptians maintained that astrology and alchemy were bestowed on man by the benevolence of the gods.

DIVINE PLANETS
In antiquity, particularly among the Babylonians and Egyptians, the planets were regarded as deities.

DIVINE SIGNS
In Egyptian astrology, the four fixed signs of the Zodiac were termed Sons of Horus.

DIVINE SPIRIT
In ancient Egypt and in Babylonia the spirit of the cult-god was indwelling in the stars.

DIVINITY OF ASTROLOGY
The ancient Egyptians claimed that astrology was bestowed on man by the benevolence of the gods.

DIVISION OF DAY
Among the ancient Babylonians the day was divided into twelve periods, each period being equivalent to two hours.

DIVORCES
Divorces based on trivialities or on estrangements take place when the luminaries are in disjunct signs or in opposition or in quartile.

DOMAL DIGNITY
Astrologically, this term describes a planet when it tenants its own sign. A planet so placed was described in ancient astrology as "domiciliated."

DOMITIAN
This Roman Emperor (61-96 A.D.) was hostile to astrologers and banished them from Rome. He was afraid of their predictions as they affected him. The astrologers had forecast the year, the exact hour, and the manner of his death. They also predicted that Domitian would die by the dagger of a freedman.

DORYPHORY

Astrologically, this is a Ptolemaic term that describes a planet which serves as a sort of bodyguard to the Sun, rising shortly before it — either in the same or the contiguous sign. The doryphory of the Moon similarly rises after it.

DRAGON'S HEAD, DRAGON'S TAIL

Astrologically, these are points or nodes in which the ecliptic is intersected by the orbits of the planets. The Dragon's Head is the point where a planet begins its northern latitude. The Dragon's Tail is a point where a planet begins its southern course.

DRYDEN, JOHN

(1631-1700). Dryden, the celebrated English poet, was deeply interested in astrology. He even cast the horoscopes of his own sons.

DUAL CHARACTER OF ASTROLOGY

In antiquity, particularly in the Middle East, astrology was not only a science, despite its variable potency in predictions and similar astrological assurances, but a religious faith as well — beyond rational calculation, beyond hazards and suppositions.

DUMB SIGNS

Astrologically, these are mute signs: Cancer, Scorpio, Pisces. One of them on the Ascendant and Mercury afflicted, or Mercury aspected by a malefic posited in one of them is cited as the possible cause of speech impediment.

DYSIS

In astrological terminology, the dysis is the western angle or point of setting.

EAGLE

Astrologically, a small constellation located approximately Capricorn twenty-nine degrees. Sometimes called the Vulture.
The Eagle is frequently associated with the sign Scorpio. By the Greeks and Persians the Eagle was held sacred to the Sun and Jupiter.

EARLIEST ASTROLOGERS

The earliest Egyptian astrologers to be mentioned in records were the 'godlike' Petosiris and Necepso. Petosiris is believed to have been a king and Necepso a priest in the reign of Rameses II (1292-1225 B.C.). The two astrologers are mentioned by both Greek and Roman writers: Athenaeus, Aristophanes, Pliny the Elder, Galen, Juvenal.

EARTH SIGNS

The signs of the Earth Triplicity: Taurus, Virgo, Capricorn. The ancients symbolized these types by the Earth element, because of their predominant Earthiness or practicality.

EBERTIN, ELSBETH

Frau Ebertin, a well-known German astrologer, had formerly

been a graphologist. She produced an astrological prediction regarding Hitler and foretold his rise to Führer.

Her reputation spread and she became an influential personality, and made a significant impact on the German public.

ECCLESIASTICS AND ASTROLOGY
In the Middle Ages the clerics looked on astrological studies as a link with occult and Satanic practices.

ECLIPSE
In antiquity, an eclipse of the Sun or of the Moon was ominous for mankind. It generally portended catastrophes upon the earth.

ECLIPSE OF THALES
May, 28, 585 B.C. Predicted by Thales of Miletus. It stopped a battle in the war between the Medes and the Lydians. Among other historic eclipses were: eclipse which occurred at noon in in the first year of the Peloponnesian War, when several stars became visible: traditional date — August 3, 432 B.C.: eclipse which occurred when Agathocles, King of Syracuse, was sailing with his fleet toward Africa, on August 15, 310 B.C.

On the day of a solar eclipse, March 7, 51 B.C., Julius Caesar crossed the Rubicon.

ECLIPTIC
Astrologically, the most significant part that gives the astrologer his answers to his calculations is the ecliptic or the Sun's trajectory. It rises in the East at the moment of birth or of any undertaking which is subjected to the casting of a horoscope.

ECLIPTIC: VIA SOLIS, THE SUN'S PATH
The Sun's apparent orbit or path around the Earth. Or the orbit of the Earth as viewed from the Sun. So named because it is along this path, at the points where it intersects the Equator, that the eclipses occur.

EFFECTS OF CELESTIAL MOTIONS
Ptolemy in his *Tetrabiblos* declares that the motions of the stars and planets through the sky often signify weather conditions whereby mundane affairs too are affected.

EGYPT
Ancient Egypt had the most profound knowledge and interest in astrology. One of the most eminent authorities on Egyptian astrology was Franz Cumont (1868-1947), Professor at the University of Ghent, in Belgium. He is the author of a study entitled *L'Egypte des Astrologues*.

It was anciently believed, on the other hand, that the Egyptians acquired their astrological knowledge from the Ethiopians.

EGYPTIAN AFTERLIFE
In the tombs of Egyptian kings' papyri have been found inscribed with astronomical and astrological information as guides in the journey through the afterlife.

EGYPTIAN ASTROLOGY
In ancient Egypt Virgo, the zodiacal sign, represented the goddess Isis. It was also a hermaphroditic symbol.

EGYPTIAN CALENDAR
In 4241 B.C. the Egyptian calendar was introduced. It consisted of twelve months of thirty days each, plus five feast days.

EGYPTIAN PROCESSIONS
In the religious processions of the Egyptian cults, astrologers were invariably participants.

EGYPTIAN PROGNOSTICATION
Those who have most advanced this faculty of the art of prognostication, the Egyptians, have entirely united medicine with astronomical prediction. — Ptolemy, *Tetrabiblos*.

EIGHTEENTH CENTURY
The eighteenth century in Europe was particularly interested, in a general sense, in astrological predictions.

This interest was stimulated by the almanacs, presenting detailed astrological forecasts, that were published from the beginning of the seventeenth century by the Stationers' Company of London.

Among popular almanacs of this type were the *Speculum Anni, Merlinus Liberatus.*

The most appealing was *Old Moore's.*

EIGHTH HOUSE
The Eighth House is the House of Death. It belongs to the sign of Scorpio.

ELECTRONICS
There is currently a movement to apply electronics to astrological techniques. With the aid of computers it is thought that horoscopes may be determined with the utmost precision.

ELEVENTH HOUSE
This term, astrologically, refers to loyalty, to friends. It is governed by the sign of Aquarius.

EL HAKIM
An ancient Persian court astrologer. Author of a treatise called, in its Latin title, *Iudicia Gjaspis*, The Opinions of Gjamash. Gjamash was his variant name.

EMBOLISMIC MONTH
Astrologically, this denotes embolismic lunation. An intercalary month used in some ancient calendars, to preserve a seasonal relationship between the lunar and solar calendar.

ENGLAND
In 1825, in England, the Vagrancy Act outlawed all practitioners of astrology.

ENOCH
This Biblical patriarch had a reputation in the Middle Ages for a profound knowledge of astrology.

EPACT
This term, of Greek origin, is applied to a number that indicates the Moon's age on the first day of the year. As the common solar year is 365 days, and the lunar year 354 days, the difference of eleven indicates that if a new moon falls on January 1st in any year, it will be eleven days old on the first day of the next year, and twenty-two days old on the first of the third year. Hence the epacts of those years are numbers eleven and twenty-two.

EPHEMERAL MAP
A map erected for the time of an event, to be judged by Horary Astrology.

EPHEMERIDES
These are tables for finding the position of the sun, the moon, and the planets at a person's birth. These tables are used in casting horoscopes.

EPHEMERIS
Plural: Ephemerides. An almanac listing the ephemeral or rapidly changing position which each of the solar system bodies will occupy on each day of the year: their longitude, latitude, declination, and similar astronomical phenomena. The astronomer's Ephemeris lists these positions in heliocentric terms: that of the astrologer in geocentric terms. A set of Ephemerides which includes the year of the native's birth is essential in the erection of a horoscope. Ephemerides were first devised by astrologers to facilitate the erection of a horoscope. Finally, when they became in common use to navigators and astronomers, they were given official recognition and issued as the Nautical Almanac. The oldest almanac in the British Museum bears the date 131. It is said that Columbus navigated by the aid of an astrologer's Ephemeris.

EPIC HOROSCOPE
The famous ancient epic poem of India, the Ramayana, was composed by Valmiki, who expounded the horoscope of the divine Rama.

ESAHADDON
An ancient Assyrian king who belongs in the seventh century B.C. He had his own court astrologers.

ESSAY ON ASTROLOGY
Lucian, the Greek satirist who belongs in the second century A.D., has an essay on astrology, its history, and on the astrological interpretations of the ancient myths.

ESSENTIAL DIGNITIES
A planet in a sign in which it is strengthened is one of its Essential Dignities. The Essential Dignities are:
1. When a planet is in sign of which it is the Ruler, when it is said to be in its own sign, or in its domal dignity. It is ambiguous to call this its House-position. If the sign which a planet rules is on the cusp of the House to which the planet is posited, the planet is the Lord of the House: but the strength as such depends on its Essential Dignity by virtue of its sign placement. Some astrologers consider that placement in any other sign of the same element as that of which it is the Ruler confers a degree of Dignity.
2. When it is posited in the sign in which it is said to be exalted, wherein its strength is augmented and its virtues magnified. A planet in its Exaltation is only slightly less favorably placed than when it is in its own sign.
3. According to ancient astrology, the placement of a planet in the same Triplicity as that of which it is the Ruler, in the same Term, or in the same Face, was considered to be Essential Dignities of varying degree.

ESTE
In the ancient Egyptian temple of Este, the Temple of the

East, there has been unearthed a pictorial representation of the zodiacal signs.

ESTIMATES OF THE TETRABIBLOS
Ptolemy's astrological survey, entitled the *Tetrabiblos*, treats, in theoretical terms, the value of the art and the possible benefits it can confer when it is properly applied.
There follows a collection of ancient sources and comments relating to astrological practices.
In conclusion, there is an explanation of the laws of nature, in so far as antiquity could know the underlying associations between the celestial bodies and the terrestrial earth.

ETHIOPIANS
The Ethiopians were credited with having been the first to practice astrology. They were said to have transmitted this knowledge to the Egyptians.

EULOGY OF ASTROLOGERS
Vitruvius, the Roman writer on architecture, who belongs in the first century A.D., declared in the introduction to his treatise that the learning of the astrologers merited the admiration of all men.

EXALTATION
A term used in astrology to denote the position of greatest influence of the Sun and the Moon and the other planets.

EXAMINATION OF ZODIAC
According to Ptolemy in his *Tetrabiblos*, the first consideration in erecting a horoscope is the position of the Zodiac.

EXCLUSIVE ART
For many centuries, particularly in antiquity, astrology was considered a royal art, practiced by kings and emperors, and affecting only such personalities as were of the highest poli-

tical or social level. It was an art associated with dukes and princes, with popes and prelates.

EXPULSION
In 52 A.D. all astrologers were expelled from Rome under a decree of the Emperor Claudius.

EXPULSION OF CHALDEANS
The Chaldaei — the Latin term used by the Romans to designate the astrologers who crowded into Rome to sell their oracular wares, were repeatedly expelled from the city by the Senate and the first Roman Emperors. But they persistently reappeared in the Roman capital.

FACE

(1) As employed by Ptolemy, a planet in a House that is distant counter-clockwise from the Moon, or clockwise from the Sun by the same number of Houses as the Sign, is in its Face. This means that Mercury is in its Face when in a House preceding that of the Moon, or following that of the Sun; Venus, when two Houses preceding or following; Mars, three Houses; Jupiter, four Houses; or Saturn, five Houses — duplicating in Houses from the actual Sun and Moon position, the scheme of Sign-Rulership from Cancer and Leo, around to Capricorn and Aquarius.

(2) James Wilson gives a series of 10 degree Faces which are merely the scheme of Decanates with their Rulers according to one of the ancient systems. Since this is only a distinction of terms without a difference in meaning, the employment of the term Face in this sense is confusing and unnecessary.

(3) Alan Leo defines a Face as one of a series of 5 degree subdivisions of a Sign. His fondness for symbolism is reflected in the interpretations which he applies to those who have a rising Degree in each of the 72 arcs in this series of what might better be called demi-Decans.

FAMILIARITY
A term used by Ptolemy to indicate an aspect or parallel between two bodies: or their mutual disposition, as when each is in the other's sign or house.

FANCIFUL ASTROLOGERS
In the periodical literature of the eighteenth and early nineteenth century, devoted to astrological practices, many astrologers wrote under pen names such as Mercurius, Astrologus, Tarantobobus.

FATALISM
Francis Bacon declared, with reference to the doctrines of the early astrologers regarding predestination:
> There is no fatal necessity in the stars, and this, the more prudent astrologers have constantly allowed.

In the ancient pagan cults, belief in astrology posited the dogma of fatalism. This was the case notably among the Romans.

FATE
The belief that astrological influences determine Man's fate, that the issues of all events are predetermined, and that no effort can avail him to alter it, is an extreme view to which few modern astrologers subscribe, since it would deprive his active will and effort of mind of any effective part in determining the events of his life. The doctrine of Fate should therefore be regarded as somewhat misleading on the ground that it is in conflict with the modern concept of Man as a free moral agent.

FEMININE SIGNS
These are the even numbered signs: Taurus, Cancer, Virgo, Scorpio, Capricorn, Pisces.

FICINO, MARSILIO
(1433-1499) Famous Italian philosopher and astrologer. Dominican monk. Developed a theory that postulated a relationship

between music and the celestial bodies. He was attached to the court of Cosimo and of Lorenzo de Medici.

FIERY CHARACTER
The fiery nature of Mars was implicit in his Greek name of Pyrois.

FIFTH HOUSE
This term refers to the family and to occupations. It is governed by the sign of Leo.

FIGURE
An astrological or celestial figure, variously called Geniture, Map, Scheme, Chart, Theme, Mirror of Heaven, Nativity, Horoscope, as cast, erected or drawn by modern astrologers. It consists of a circle of the heavens, representing the 360 degrees of the Earth's orbit, divided into twelve arcs — resembling a wheel of twelve spokes.

FIRE SIGNS
This expression is applied to the inspirational signs: Aries, Leo, Sagittarius.

FIRMICUS MATERNUS, JULIUS
A Roman writer who flourished in the fourth century A.D. He is the author of an astrological treatise in eight books.

FIRST HOUSE
This term refers to the house of life. It is governed by the sign of Aries.

FIRST POINT
This expression refers to zero degrees Aries. From this point longitude is reckoned along the ecliptic, and right ascension along the celestial equator.

FIVE PLANETS
The five planets were known in Babylonian astrology as the five interpreters.

FLEXED
This is an alternate tern for the mutable signs. This term is preferred by some modern astrologers.

FLOOD
Seneca, the Roman Stoic philosopher (c. 4 B.C. - 65 A.D.,) asserted that when all the stars are in conjunction in Capricorn a deluge will occur.

FLUDD, ROBERT
(1574-1637) English physician and mystic. Author of a treatise in defense of the Black Arts. He also wrote *Utriusque Cosmi maioris et minoris Historia*, 1619. In his *Integrum Morborum Mysterium*, The Complete Secret of Diseases, he conceived sickness as the result of demoniac forces.

FOHI
A legendary Chinese ruler, called The Divine Emperor. He is traditionally credited with granting mankind a knowledge of divination with the aid of the planets.

FONTENELLE, BERNARD
(1657-1757) French man of letters. Among his works is *La Comète*, treating astrology in a farcical manner.

FORECAST OF WEALTH
Thales, the ancient Greek philosopher, wished to prove that a philosopher too could be wealthy, if he so desired. He cast a horoscope of the olive crop, and by buying up the oil presses he quickly amassed a fortune.

FORMAL ASTROLOGY
At the university of Prague, which was established by the Emperor Charles V (1316-1378,) one of the disciplines in the academic course was astrology.

FORMAN, Dr.
An astrologer and magician who belongs in the seventeenth

century. He practiced image magic at the court of King James VI of Scotland.

FORTIFIED
This term denotes strongly placed: either elevated, in a congenial sign, or well-aspected.

FORTITUDE
An ancient term denoting a quality or strength possessed by a planet when posited in its own sign or that of its exaltation.

FORTUNA, PARS FORTUNAE
The Part of Fortune. One of the Arabian Points. A point that bears the same relation to the rising degree that the Moon bears to the Sun. It occupies the same house-position in a Figure based on a birth-moment, that the Moon tenants in a solar figure. Its symbol, a cross within a circle, $\oplus$, is utilized by astronomers to represent the earth. It is the ancient Chinese symbol Tien, a field used by the Egyptians to signify territory. It is generally considered that the house-position of Fortuna is an indication of the department of life that will most readily contribute to the financial welfare of the native.

FOUR-FOOTED SIGNS
These are: Aries, Taurus, Leo, Sagittarius, Capricorn: sometimes termed "animal signs." One whose ascendant is posited in one of these signs was anciently presumed to possess some of the qualities of that particular animal: as bold as a lion, lustful as a goat, etc.

FOURTH AGE
According to Ptolemy, the Sun, which is the supreme planet, controls the fourth age, approximately from twenty to forty. The Sun also rules gold and the lion.

FOURTH HOUSE
This term refers to the house of children and of home. It is governed by the sign of Cancer.

FRANCE
In medieval France, most rulers had their own court astrologers. John II, for instance, who belongs in the fourteenth century, had several astrologers to chart and predict the outcome of his wars.

FREDERICK II
(1194-1250) King of Sicily and Naples. He had several astrologers attached to his court. His interest in the subject of astrology was so keen that he had the *Almagest* translated from Arabic into Latin.

FRIENDLY PLANETS
Ptolemy appeared to believe that those planets which have rulership, exaltation, or triplicity in each other's Signs should be classed as friendly planets. Other authorities class them as follows:

Sun — unfriendly only to Saturn.

Moon — unfriendly only to Mars and Saturn.

Mars — friendly to Venus only.

Jupiter — unfriendly only to Mars.

Saturn — friendly only to the Sun, Mercury, and Jupiter.

Just how Saturn can be friendly to the Sun when the latter is unfriendly to him is nowhere explained, and James Wilson says the entire concept is nonsense. A little thought, however, will discern its basic truth when the qualities of the various vibrations are considered. With regard to the Sun-Saturn objection, what Ptolemy probably meant was Saturn's application in beneficent aspect to the solar orb, for no one can deny that a sextile or trine from Saturn to the Sun mightily strengthens the latter and agrees with its purpose.

GAIO

Maestro Gaio (1388-1460) was a Rabbi in Rome. He was a noted physician and astrologer as well: a combination of disciplines that was usual in the Middle Ages and later. Gaio wrote a fanciful poem on a journey among the celestial bodies.

GALACTIC CENTRE

The gravitational centre around which the Sun revolves. Astrology has hypothetically placed this at zero degrees Capricorn, which is exactly confirmed by recently published results of calculations of spectroscopic radial velocity measurements as well as calculations by the parallax method of determining proper motion.

GALACTIC LATITUDE

The angular distance of a celestial body from the median plane of the Milky Way.

GALEN

Greek physician who flourished in the second century A.D. Wrote numerous treatises on medical matters, of which about 100 are extant. Two of his works are treatises on astrological medicine.

One deals with the Critical Days of a disease as affected by the Moon. The other work is entitled *Prognostication of Disease by Astrology.*

GALLIC ASTROLOGY
In Gaul, under the priestly Druids, astrology was regularly practiced and continued to flourish into the late Roman Empire.

GARNETT, RICHARD
(1835-1906) Eminent English man of letters, attached to the British Museum. He displayed a considerable interest in astrology. He also published a number of stories on the subject.

GAURICE, LUC
Italian mathematician and astrologer who belongs to the end of the fifteenth century. He was attached to the Prince of Bologna: also made predictions for Henry II of France.

GAUTIER OF METZ
Flourished in the thirteenth century. Author of a poem entitled *Imago Mundi,* which contains an exposition of astrology.

GEMINI
The Twins. The third, northern sign of the zodiac. It is of dual significance, creative and destructive. In occultism it symbolizes the twin souls. Kabalistically, the sign represents the arms and hands of the grand man of the universe, and accordingly the executive principle of humanity.

GENETHLIALOGY
The branch of astrology that deals with the birth of individuals, whereby a judgment is formed of a person's characteristics from a map of the heavens cast for his given birth moment.

GENITURE
A birth or genesis. This term is approximately synonymous with nativity, referring to the subject whose birth horoscope is under

consideration. A reasonable discrimination would be to employ nativity with reference to the person and geniture with reference to the configurations which show in his birth map. Ptolemy mentions a Lord of the Geniture in referring to the ruling planet in a given horoscope of birth.

GEOARC
A term applied to one of the house divisions of a map erected for a given moment, when there is under consideration the effect upon an individual at a given point on the earth's periphery of his motion around the earth's centre, in the earth's daily rotation. The same subdivision of the same map is called a heliarc, when there is under consideration the effect based on the actual motions in orbit around the Sun, of all the planets, including the earth.

GEOPONICA
This is a Greek treatise on agriculture that belongs in the Middle Ages. Among other topics, it deals with astrological forecasts.

GILGAMESH
The heroic life of Gilgamesh, Sumerian king of Urak, is related in twelve Babylonian cuneiform clay tablets. Each tablet deals with one incident in his life, and each incident involves one of the twelve signs of the zodiac.

GIUNTINI, FRANCISCO
(1522-1590) Italian astrologer. Author of *Speculum Astrologiae*, a collection of horoscopes of eminent men.

GIVER OF LIFE
The hyleg, or significator that holds the vital prerogative.

GNOSTICS
The Gnostics were a sect that broke away from Christianity and established theosophical systems of their own. They flourished chiefly during the second and third centuries A.D. The Gnostics conceived the seven planets as powers that governed the world.

GRADIAL, TRANSIT, ARC OF
A term that indicates the arc a planet traverses from its earth position to its progressed position, when in any given year it is activated by a major transit through the arc.

GRAND TRINE
Two planets trine to each other, both of which are trined by a third planet.

GREATEST ASTROLOGER
In antiquity, Berosus, a priest of the god Baal, was the first and regarded as the greatest astrologer among the Chaldeans. There was a legend that the majority of his prognostications were verified.

GREAT YEAR
The first year of the universe, the initiation of the zodiac and the planets, was known as the *Annus Magnus,* The Great Year. This is a period of some 26,000 years, divided into twelve parts corresponding to the twelve zodiacal signs.

GREEK HOROSCOPE
The British Museum has preserved an ancient Greek horoscope. Some authorities, however, assert that the horoscope started in Egypt.

GREEK MYTHOLOGY
Lucian, the Greek satirist, who flourished in the second century A.D., contended that the Greek myths had no reality and were merely astrological fantasies.

GREGORIAN CALENDAR
On October 5, 1582 (old style, according to the Julian calendar,) it was decreed by Pope Gregory VIII that this date should be changed to October 15 (new style). This latter date is the beginning of the Gregorian calendar.

GUARDED
This term is applied to one or more elevated planets guarded on the East by the Sun and on the West by the Moon.

GUY MANNERING
In this novel by Sir Walter Scott, the subject is based on an astrological issue, the genethliacal horoscope of an infant.

HABITAT OF PLANETS
Each planet was assigned to one of the elements. The Moon was the earth, Mercury was water. Jupiter was the air: Saturn was water. The sphere of the stars was the celestial earth.

HADRIAN
The Roman Emperor Hadrian erected a building at Jerusalem which was called Dodecapylon, or the Temple of the Twelve Gates — an evident reference to the twelve houses of the Sun. He also divided the city into twelve areas: in relation to the number of planets and planetary spheres.

HADRIAN'S DIARY
The Roman Emperor Hadrian was so dedicated to astrological concepts that, after consultation of the stars, he wrote a kind of diary, a blue-print of his own life, including the time of his death.

HAPPY MARRIAGE
According to Ptolemy's *Tetrabiblos*, marriages endure if in both genitures the luminaries harmonize in aspect, in trine or sextile with each other.

HAYZ

In Horary Questions, this term denotes a masculine diurnal planet above the earth in a day figure, and a feminine nocturnal planet under the earth in a night figure. This is called a Dignity of I degree, and is reckoned fortunate. The Arabs did not conceive a perfect Hayz except when the masculine planet was in a male sign, or the feminine planet in a female sign. A masculine planet in a male sign under the earth by day was considered to be only in his light, and the person denoted by it to be in a state of contentment.

HEAVEN

Heaven is divided in twelve compartments, each marked by one of the twelve signs of the zodiac.

HEAVENLY OMENS

In Shakespeare's *Julius Caesar*, Act 2, Calpurnia, Caesar's wife, tries to dissuade her husband from going to the Senate. Malefic omens, she declares, have been observed:

A lioness hath whelped in the streets,
And graves have yawned and yielded up their dead;
Fierce fiery warriors fought upon the clouds,
In ranks and squadrons and right form of war,
Which drizzled blood upon the Capitol;
The noise of battle hurtled in the air.
Horses did neigh and dying men did groan,
And ghosts did shriek and squeal about the streets ...
When beggars die, there are no comets seen;
The heavens themselves blaze forth the death of princes.

HELIACAL RISING

This term denotes a rising of the Sun. When a planet or a star, after it has been hidden by the Sun's rays, becomes again visible, that is a heliacal rising.

HELIACAL SETTING

This expression is applied when a star is overtaken by the Sun and is lost in its rays. The heliacal rising or setting of the Moon occurs when it is within 17 degrees of the Sun: other stars and planets, when within 30 degrees distance.

HELIOCENTRIC ASTROLOGY
In this type of astrology the astrological interpretations are based on a Figure in which the solar system bodies are located according to their heliocentric longitudes.

HELIOCENTRIC LONGITUDE AND LATITUDE
This is based on the Sun as the centre. The Nautical Almanac gives the heliocentric positions of all celestial bodies. The astrologer's Ephemeris is now made from the Nautical Almanac by reducing these positions to their geocentric equivalent.

HENRY II
(1154-1189) King of England. He was the patron of the scholars of his time, notably Geoffrey of Monmouth. He also took a great interest in astrology.

HERALD OF ASTROLOGY
An English periodical devoted to astrology, published in 1832 and later changed to *Zadkiel's Almanac*. Zadkiel, or Zadkiel the Seer, was himself an English astrologer whose actual name was Morrison.

HERBAIS DE THUN, CHARLES DE, VICOMTE
Belgian astrologer who belongs in the nineteenth century. Author of *Encyclopédie du Mouvement astrologue de langue française*.

HERBARIUM OF APULEIUS
A treatise attributed to Apuleius, who belongs in the second century A.D. The work deals with herbal medicine and the relation of herbs to the study of astrology.

HESIOD
Hesiod, the Greek poet who flourished in the ninth century B.C., was, according to Plutarch, the Greek biographer, knowledgeable in astrological lore.

HEXAGON
A line drawn between every second zodiacal sign forms a hexagon or sextile. The sextile is regarded astrologically as favorable.

HEYDON, JOHN
An English astrologer who flourished in the seventeenth century. He also wrote on the occult arts, and was himself a Rosicrucian.

HIMMLER
Himmler, one of Hitler's chief associates, was deeply involved in astrology. The interest in astrology, in fact, was pervasive among the Nazi leaders. More extensively, it has now spread throughout Germany.

HINDU ASTROLOGY
In Hindu astrology the seven suns of the Dragon of Wisdom control the destiny of the world.

HINDU TEXTS
Many astrological treatises were anciently composed by the sages of India, the Maharishis.

HIPPARCHUS
Hipparchus, who belongs in the second century B.C., was a Greek astronomer and astrologer. According to the Roman encyclopedist Pliny the Elder, Hipparchus convincingly expounded the doctrine of the relation between man and the stars, and the affinity between the human soul and the heavenly bodies.

HIPPOCRATES
The Greek physician who belongs in the fourth century B.C. He is said to have used astrological techniques in his medical treatments.

HIPPOLYTUS
Greek scholar who belongs in the third century A.D. He conceived astrology as impracticable in its operations.

HISTORICAL INTERPRETATIONS
Attempts have been made by some practicing astrologers to relate the motions and the traditional properties and influences of the heavenly bodies to historical events. Analyses have been made, *post factum,* of the coincidences between mundane events in their entire historical sequence.

HITLER
In addition to his ailurophobia, his fear of cats, Hitler had a strong belief in the virtues of astrology. He had his own astrologer, who charted the daily course for Hitler, in terms of the dominant immediate and prospective mutual relations of the planets and their energies.

HOMODROMI
This term, of Greek origin, means fellow-runners. It is applied to the internal or variously called minor or inferior planets Mercury and Venus, which have a maximum elongation from the Sun of approximately 28 degrees and 46 degrees respectively.

HONORS
Honors refer to the Sun and Midheaven and their radical aspects, indicating the degrees of fame and honor to which a person is predestined. The luminaries in an angle and well-aspected are a sign of high honors. Jupiter rising, or in the Midheaven, shows a high degree of prestige. Saturn similarly placed denies credit and renown, however much deserved. Rising planets show aspirations to honors and high ambition, but the outcome of such aspirations depends on which planet first culminates. If the majority of the planets are oriental to the Moon, the native will arrive at authority and accumulate wealth. In modern astrology, the term is rare.

German astrological clock.

Old Arabic Zodiac.

HORARY CYCLES
The arcs or circles, in which the planets appear to move around the earth by virtue of the earth's diurnal revolution. The cycles are either diurnal or nocturnal.

HORARY FIGURE
When a person is ill, a prognosis of the condition is derived by setting up a horary figure at the moment of the sickness. This figure is called decumbiture, which means: a lying down.

HORIMEA
This term refers to the rays of the Hyleg after it has passed the Midheaven.

HOROSCOPE
The rising sign of the zodiac in which the degree of the ecliptic lies is called the horoscope. Popularly, a horoscope is a diagram showing the relative positions of the planets and signs of the zodiac and providing a basis for predictions concerning an individual. Hundreds of thousands of Americans now buy computer-produced 'personal' horoscopes for about $20.00 each.

HOROSCOPE ET ASTRES
This is the title of a French astrological periodical that has a wide national circulation.

HOROSCOPIC POINT
Difficulty often arises, according to Ptolemy in his *Tetrabiblos*, with regard to the first and most important fact, that is, the fraction of the hour of the birth; for in general only observation by means of horoscopic astrolabes at the time of birth can scientific observers give the minute of the hour.

HOROSCOPUS
In ancient Egyptian religious processionals, one of the participants was the Horoscopus, who was versed in the treatises of Hermes Trismegistus, Hermes the Thrice Greatest, who in

the Egyptian mind was identified with the Egyptian god Thoth, the master of all knowledge.

HOUSE
Every planet has two houses, one of the day, the other of the night.

HOUSE OF LIFE
This refers to all the influences, favorable or malefic, that affect the life of a person.

HOUSE OF SCIENCE
In the eleventh century, in Cairo, the Caliph Al Hakim founded this academic institution in which astronomy and astrology were among the disciplines taught.

HOUSES, CLASSIFICATION OF
Houses are classed as follows:
Individual or Life Houses: 1, 5, 9, representing respectively the body, soul, and spirit: the Trinity of Life.
Temporal or Possessive Houses: representing the temporal status of the native: 2, possessions and property: 6, comforts: 10, honor and credit position in society: the Trinity of Wealth.
Relative or Association Houses: relating to human relationships: 3, ties of consanguinity: 7, conjugal ties: 11, friendship: the Trinity of Association.
Terminal or Psychic Houses: referring to eventualities particularly the termination of conditions in the native's life: 4, environment in each period of life: 8, influence of others: 12, hindering influences: the Trinity of Psychism.

HOUSES, GROUPING OF
Houses may be grouped by direction:
Eastern Houses: Those in the eastern half of the Figure, containing planets rising toward the Midheaven: that is the third, second, first, twelfth, eleventh, tenth. Of these, the three above the horizon — containing planets which, moving clockwise

against the order of the signs, are passing away from the horizon toward their culmination at the Midheaven — are considered to confer upon these planets added strength 'by position.'

Western Houses: Houses in the western half of the Figure — fourth, fifth, sixth, seventh, eighth, ninth. Posited in these Houses, malefic planets are said to be strengthened and benefic planets weakened — particularly regarding their influence on the native's health.

Oriental Houses: Houses which extend clockwise from the horizon to the meridian: to twelfth, eleventh, tenth, sixth, fifth, fourth.

Occidental Houses: Houses which extend clockwise from the meridian to the horizon: the ninth, eighth, seventh, third, second, first.

HUDIBRAS

Samuel Butler (c. 1612-1680), English satirist, author of the mock-heroic poem *Hudibras*, which contains astrological allusions:

As is men from the stars did suck Old-age, diseases, and ill-luck. Wit, folly, honor, virtue, vice, Trade, travel, women, claps and dice; And draw with the first air they breathe, Battle, and murther, sudden death.

HUXLEY, ALDOUS

In his novel *Crome Yellow* the English novelist has one of his characters, Priscilla, cast horoscopes of horses and of the players on football teams:

Most of Priscilla's days were spent casting the horoscope of horses, and she invested her money scientifically, as the Stars dictated. She betted on football too, and had a large notebook in which she registered the horoscopes of all the players in all the teams of the League.

HYLEG

This term means *the giver of life*. It denotes a planet so located as to have influence upon the longevity of the native. It is one of the most complex and controversial subjects in the field of astrology, but it has fallen more or less in disfavor as a result of the concept that any attempt to predict the time of death is now considered unethical. The strongest planet that occupied one of the aphetic places became Hyleg and was considered to be the Apheta, the giver of life. When it had progressed to an aspect to the place of the Anareta, the taker-away of life, the native was presumed to have run his span of life.

HYMN TO THE SUN
Julian the Apostate, the Christian Roman Emperor who turned to paganism, belongs in the fourth century A.D. He is the author of a Hymn to the Sovereign Sun, which is packed with astrological allusions.

HYPOGEON
This expression, of Greek origin, denotes *under the earth*. In astrology, it generalizes the lower heaven: it includes the nadir, the *imum coeli* and the Fourth House.

IAMBLICHUS
Neoplatonic philosopher who belongs in the fourth century A.D. He postulates the practice of astrology, based on revelation, and also on the knowledge transmitted by the Chaldeans.

IBN SHAPRUT
(915-990) Jewish physician and astrologer at court of the Caliph of Bagdad. He was one of the teachers at the Academy of Cordova in Spain.

IBN VERGA
Astrologer and Kabalist who flourished in Spain in the fifteenth century.

I CHING
An ancient Chinese treatise which means *The Book of Changes*. It is probably the oldest Chinese literary text, dating possibly from the third millennium B.C. It treats of divination by certain combinations of symbols.

IMPEDED, IMPEDITED
These two synonymous terms refer to a luminary or planet when

badly aspected, especially by the malefics. The terms are also used of the Moon when passing to a conjunction, square, or opposition to the Sun, Mars, or Saturn. The Moon when impedited by the Sun at birth was anciently said to produce a blemish in or near the eye.

IMPERFECT SIGNS: BROKEN SIGNS
These signs are: Leo, Scorpio, Pisces.

IMPORTANT CAUSE
The most effective consideration of a predicted event depends on the conjunctions of the Sun and Moon at eclipse and on the motions of the stars.

IMUM COELI
This Latin expression means: the lowest heaven. Astrologically the North Angle or cusp of the Fourth House.

INCONJUNCT
This term means: dissociate. A planet is inconjunct when it forms no aspect and is not in parallel of declination or mutual disposition to another planet. Dissociate was formerly applied to the 150 degrees or Quincunx aspect, which was regarded as inconsequential. Now it is applied to any two signs or houses which have no familiarity with each other, that is, those which bear a twelfth, second, sixth, and eighth house relationship, as Taurus with Aries, Gemini, Libra, and Sagittarius.

INDIA
In India the impact of astrology has long pervaded and still pervades — all levels of society, government officials, business men, peasants, clerical workers.
A husband and wife consulted an astrologer when desiring to have a child. Intercourse was conditioned, on the astrologer's advice, by the conjunction of the Moon with a male planet, Mars or the Sun.

Astrology, it may be added, was practiced in India thousands of years before the compilation of the Vedas.

INDIGENOUS ASTROLOGY
It is contended that Hindu astrology is an indigenous science and does not owe anything to the Greeks or the Arabs. Hindu astrology derives solely from its own antique native sources.

INFERIOR PLANETS
These are the minor planets, those whose orbits are within that of the earth, namely, Mercury and Venus.

INFERNAL POWERS
St. Augustine (354-430), the famous Church Father and philosopher, accepted the precision of astrological predictions, but he contended that there was a Satanic agency that operated intrusively.

INFLUENCE IN INDIA
In a general sense, astrology has for centuries exerted and still exerts a powerful influence on all levels of society in India.

INFLUENCE OF BABYLONIA
Babylonian astronomy and astrology exercised a powerful influence on the Semitic cults of the Middle East and also on the Persian cult of Mithra.

INFLUENCE OF MOON
The Moon, which rules Cancer, exerts an influence on the tides, and on women's menstrual periods. It is also significant for those proposing marriage. In the Middle Ages, the Moon was considered as a factor in mental conditions. The term *lunacy* is an inheritage of that belief.

INFLUENCE OF VENUS
If Venus rules action, her subjects deal with dyes and wines, spices and clothing, unguents and colors and drugs.

INFORTUNES
This term is applied to Mars and Saturn.

INGRESS
This term applies to the entry of any orbital body into a sign or a quadrant. The Sun makes an ingress into the cardinal signs at the equinoxes and solstices. The planets also have their ingresses into the various signs, which result in certain alterations of their influence.

INITIATING SIGNS
The first sign of each season of the year: the cardinal signs: Aries, Cancer, Libra, Capricorn, characterized by a constant state of mobilization for action.

INSPIRATIONAL NATURES
This expression refers to the quality of sensory receptivity and reaction that characterizes those born with the Sun in Aries, Leo, and Sagittarius — respectively, the initiative, executive, and deductive type of the inspirational group.

INTELLECTUAL NATURES
This expression refers to a quality of sensory receptivity through the mind that characterizes those born with the Sun in Libra, Aquarius, and Gemini — respectively, the initiative, executive, and deductive types of the intellectual group.

INTERCEPTED HOUSE
A House in which a sign is contained wholly within the House, which sign does not appear upon either cusp of the House. An intercepted House is generally either preceded or followed by one that has the same sign on both the cusps. The affairs of an intercepted House are generally complicated and the planets therein are of more than average importance.

INTEREST IN ASTROLOGY

In contemporary times all phases of astrology have caught and held the interest of people at many social levels. This interest involves scholars, statesmen, writers, professional men, and the average citizen. In Germany there is a great resurgence of astrological concern. In France and in England the impact has spread in all social directions, while in the United States there is a continuous adherence if not devotion to the possibilities of astrological impacts.

INTEREST IN PREDICTION

Francis Bacon's (1561-1626) interest in astrological principles is shown in his *Essay on Prophecy*.

INTERPOLATION

This term is applied to computing a planet's position for a given moment between two known positions, such as the noon or midnight position prior to and subsequent to the desired moment, as taken from an Ephemeris for that year. The term is also used to compute the house cusps for an intermediate latitude between two sets of tables computed for latitudes on either side of that which the interpolation is required. In making the calculations necessary for an interpolation, use is frequently made of Tables of Diurnal Proportional Logarithms.

INTERPRETATION

This term refers to an individual judgment on the significance of a configuration of birth planets, or of transiting or progressed aspects to a birth configuration.

INTERPRETERS

The five planets were, among the Babylonians, termed Interpreters, because they predicted the fate of men and nations.

INTRODUCTION OF ZODIAC

Manetho, an Egyptian priest who belongs in the fourth century B.C. and who wrote in Greek a *History of Egypt*, was credited with the introduction of the zodiacal signs into Greece.

INVENTION OF ZODIAC
It is believed that the zodiacal system was devised by the Babylonians and dates back to the sixth century B.C.

INVOCATION TO STARS
Ye stars which are the poetry of heaven!
If in your bright leaves we seek to read the fate
Of men and empires — 'tis to be forgiven
That, in our aspirations to be great,
Our destinies o'erleap this mortal state
And claim a kindred with you: for ye are
A beauty and a mystery and create
In us such love and reverence from afar
That Life, Fame, Power and Fortune have named
    themselves a Star.

Byron

ISAAC IUDAES
A noted Jewish scholar who belongs in the seventh century. He was a physician and an astrologer. Many medical treatises appeared under his authorship, and his medical practice was based on the astrological Critical Days. He taught at the University of Kairouan.

ISAIAH
In *Isaiah* 48.13 the prophet declares: Let now the astrologers, the star-gazers, the monthly prognosticators stand up, and save thee from these things that shall come upon thee.

ISHTAR
In Babylonia the goddess Ishtar corresponded to Venus. Next to the Sun and Moon, Venus is the most powerful planet. Her signs are Libra and Taurus.

ISIDORE OF SEVILLE
Spanish scholar and encyclopedist who belongs in the seventh century A.D. He connects astrology with occult practices, but he concedes that it is to some extent a natural science.

ISLAM

Islamic culture absorbed astrology as a part of the Hellenic heritage. In the Middle Ages, when the West was affected by Islamic influences, astrology acquired an Arabic tone.

ITALY

During the Middle Ages Italy, of all the European countries, displayed the greatest interest in astrological studies, both academically and with reference to the public in general.

JACOB BEN TARIK
A Jewish scientist who established a school of astrology in Bagdad, in the eighth century A.D.

JAPAN
Astrological interest is very high in contemporary Japan. This interest includes all kinds of analyses, of the palm, of handwriting, and of phrenology. The association of professional astrologers reaches a total of some 200,000. Booths are set up in the streets to facilitate consultation of the itinerant venders of horoscopes.

JEWISH ASTROLOGERS
Many Jewish scholars in various centuries were adepts in astrological lore. Among such may be reckoned: Ibn Gabirol Jacob ibn Tarik, Abraham ben Hiyya, Abraham ibn Ezra, Isaac Arama, Abraham ibn Daud.

JOHANNES HISPALENSIS
Flourished in the middle of the twelfth century. Author of a popular treatise on astrology entitled *Epitome Totius Astrologiae*.

JOHN II
(1319-1364) King of France. In his wars with the English he enlisted the aid of professional astrologers.

JOHN OF SEVILLE
Spanish-Jewish scholar who belongs in the twelfth century. Author of a treatise on judicial astrology.

JOINED IN
This expression is applied to any body that is embraced within the orbs of any aspect to any other body: more specifically applicable to a conjunction.

JOSEPHUS
Jewish historian who belongs in the first century A.D. He was deeply interested in astrology. He regarded the stars as divine and as celestial powers.

JOYS
The planets are in their joys when they reside in the strongest and most influential Houses. For example, when Mars is in Scorpio, or the Sun is in Leo.

JUDGES OF THE WORLD
In antiquity, astrologically, these judges comprised twenty-four stars, twelve were visible, in the north. The others, the southern stars, were invisible.

JUNG, CARL G.
The famous Swiss psychologist and psychiatrist recognized some elements of validity in astrological investigations and procedures.

JUPITER
This is the greatest planet in the solar system. For several months during the year Jupiter is an all-night star. Hence it is called *the all-night watcher of the heavens.*

JUSTIN MARTYR

(second century A.D.) Of astrology, Justin wrote:
From the first invention of the hieroglyphics it was not
the vulgar, but the distinguished and select men who became initiated, in the secrets of the temples, into the science
of every kind of astrology.

JUVENAL

Decimus Iunius Iuvenalis, who belongs in the second century A.D., was the greatest Roman satirist. He inveighed against
everything that was not Roman, especially the Orient. He
particularly attacked astrology as of Eastern origin and as put
to use by Roman matrons.
Juvenal refers to astrologers from Armenia and other areas of
the Middle East who sold oracular predictions to the Roman
populace.

KABALAH

This Hebraic term, which means *Tradition,* is a Judaic mystic system, based on occult interpretations of the Bible. It also expounds an astrological system.

KAKATYCHE

This Greek term which means *ill-fortune* is applied in astrology to the Sixth House.

KANBALU

The Chinese city where Marco Polo found that the Emperor was served by some 5,000 astrologers and prognosticators.

KENKO, URABE

An occultist and prognosticator who belongs in the fourteenth century. His name signifies *of the clan of seers.*

KEPLER, JOHANNES

(1571-1630) German astronomer: discovered three laws of planetary motion. He invented the *sportula genethliaca,* instruments for the use of astrologers in casting horoscopes. He himself made many political predictions in accordance with astrological principles. He also cast the horoscopes of his personal enemies. Of his own nativity he wrote:

Jupiter nearest the nonagesimal had passed by four degrees the trine of Saturn; the Sun and Venus in conjunction were moving from the latter towards the former, nearly in sextiles with both. They were also removing from quadratures with Mars, to which Mercury was closely approaching. The moon drew near to the trine of the same planet, close to the Bull's Eye even in latitude.

KEY WORDS
Certain key words are associated with the twelve zodiacal signs, as follows:

Aries: Aspiration
Taurus: Integration
Gemini: Vivification
Cancer: Expansion
Leo: Assurance
Virgo: Assimilation
Libra: Equilibrium
Scorpio: Creativity
Sagittarius: Administration
Capricorn: Discrimination
Aquarius: Loyalty
Pisces: Appreciation

KING LEAR
In the tragedy of *King Lear*, Shakespeare has the aged monarch exclaim:

It is the stars, the stars above us govern our conditions.

KRAFFT, KARL ERNST
The official astrologer of Adolph Hitler. Krafft was a Swiss, born

in the first year of this century. Under astrological direction, he guided Hitler in his political and military decisions.

KRAFFT AND NOSTRADAMUS
It has been assumed that Karl E. Krafft, who was regarded as Hitler's astrological adviser, made use of some of the quatrains of Nostradamus, the French seer who flourished in the sixteenth century.

KRATZER, NICHOLAS
Bavarian astrologer and mathematician. He was attached to the court of Henry VIII of England. His portrait was painted by Holbein.

LAGNA SPHUTAS
This Hindu term denotes the calculating of the Ascendant.

LAYA CENTRES
Neutral states between solid, liquid, and gaseous. They are said to be governed by Saturn.

LENORMAND, MARIE ANNE ADELAIDE
She was known as the Sibyl of the Faubourg St. Germain. Her dates are: 1772-1843. As an astrologer she was frequently consulted by Napoleon. She predicted his marriage to Josephine. Among her other clients were Mme. de Stael (1766-1817), French writer, and Alexander I of Russia (1777-1825).

LEO
The Lion. The fifth, northern sign of the zodiac. It is equated with fire, with the power of the sun. In occultism, it symbolizes strength and courage. Kabalistically, it signifies the heart of the grand old man of the heavens, the fire vortex of physical ills, and the life centre of humanity.

LEO, ALAN
His actual name was W. F. Allen. He was a theosophist turned astrologer. In England, toward the close of the nineteenth century and later, he exerted considerable influence on the popular acceptance of astrology. In time, he expanded to such an extent that, to meet the demands of his numberless clients, he formed a kind of company, with the aid of associate astrologers. He published a considerable number of manuals dealing with various phases of astrological themes.

LEO VI
Byzantine Emperor from 886-911 A.D. He was interested in occultism and was also skilled in astrological techniques.

LEOVITIUS, CYPRIANUS
Noted sixteenth century astrologer of Bohemia. He wrote on eclipses and on the major conjunctions.

LIBER ASTRONOMICUS
A popular medieval treatise on astrology-astronomy by Guido Bonatti. Bonatti, a noted Italian astrologer, belongs in the thirteenth century.

LIBRA
The Balance. The seventh, southern sign of the zodiac. It symbolizes equilibrium in the material universe and in the psychic zone. Esoterically, and on the intellectual plane, it signifies external perception and intuition, united as reason and foresight. Kabalistically, it represents the kidneys and loins of the grand old man of the heavens.

LICHTENBERGER, JOHANNES
Famous German astrologer who belongs in the fifteenth century. Author of an astrological treatise.

LIGHT, COLLECTOR OF
A ponderous planet which receives the aspects of any two

significators in some of their Essential Dignities. Both must be lighter planets than the Collector itself. It denotes a mediator who will interest himself in the affairs of both parties to bring to a favorable issue a desired result which could not otherwise be achieved. It is a favorable position for reconciling differences, quarrels, lawsuits: also for bringing about marriages and various agreements.

LIGHT PLANETS
These are the Moon, Venus, Mercury, referring to their gravities and their consequent swiftness of motion. The nearer a body is to its gravitational centre, the more its motion is accelerated and its gravity proportionately diminished.

LIGHTS
This term is frequently applied to the Luminaries, the Sun and the Moon, as distinguished from the planets.

LILLY, WILLIAM
(1602-1681) English astrologer who is reputed to have predicted the Great Plague of London. Author, among other works, of *Christian Astrology,* published in 1647.

LOCI
The twelve loci are the divisions containing questions to be answered in accord with astrological calculations. They correspond to the twelve strips of the visible heaven.

LOEWE, RABBI
(1520-1609) Rabbi of Prague. Talmudical scholar, mathematician, and astrologer. Produced the automaton called The Golem.

LONGEVITY
In his *Tetrabiblos* Ptolemy expounds the astrological principles that determine the length of life of the native.

LORD

This term is often used as a synonym of Ruler. More precise terminology would indicate the Ruler of a Sign and the Lord of a House.

LORD OF THE YEAR

This is the planet that has the most Dignities in a solar revolution Figure, or in an ingress Figure to be interpreted according to the rules of Mundane Astrology.

LORENZO

Lorenzo the Magnificent (1449-1492), member of the Medici family, had a famous scholar and astrologer attached to his household. This Marsilio Ficino erected the horoscopes of Lorenzo's children.

LUCIAN

Greek satirist who belongs in the second century A.D. According to Lucian, Orpheus brought the principles of astrology from India to Greece. The planets were signified by the seven strings of his lyre.

LUMINARIES

The Lights. Said of the Sun and Moon as distinguished from the planets. It is an ancient classification hardly in keeping with the fact that the Sun is the only direct source of energy, and that the light of the Moon, like that from the planets, is reflected from the Sun. Their function with reference to solar energy is that of a filtering reflector whereby certain frequencies are absorbed by chemical properties inherent in the mass, resulting in the transmission to the Earth of an altered ray. The astrological significance, however, warrants the classification of the Sun and Moon separately from the planets, in that the Sun and Moon have to do with Man's spiritual consciousness, while the planetary influences operate through the physical mechanism. The Moon is a luminary in the biblical sense that it affords to Man 'light by night.'

LUNATION
It is approximately used as a synonym for the New Moon. Specifically, it is the precise moment of the Moon's conjunction with the Sun — a Syzgy. The New Moon falling upon sensitive points in the Figure has much signification regarding events of the ensuing month.

LUNATION, SYNODICAL
The return of the progressed Moon, after birth, to the same distance from the progressed Sun as that which the radical Moon was from the radical Sun at birth. This occurs approximately once every 29½ days.

MAGIC PLANET

In medieval times the planet Saturn was regarded as being associated with the occult arts.

MAIMONIDES

(1135-1204) Famous Spanish-Jewish philosopher. With regard to astrology, he declares:

For as much as God hath created these stars and spheres to govern the world and hath set them on high and hath imparted honor to them, and they are ministers that minister before Him, it is meet that men should laud and glorify and give them honor.

MALEFIC

This term is applied to certain planets regarded as exerting a harmful influence: chiefly Mars and Saturn. The term is also employed with reference to an inharmonious aspect with any planet, and to a conjunction with any malefic planet.

MANILIUS, MARCUS

A Roman poet who flourished in the first century A.D. He was the author of *Astronomica*, a didactic poem on the subject of astrology. Five books of the poem are extant. The themes treated include: the creation of the universe, the starry heavens and their disposition, the zodiacal signs, with their characteristics, aspects, and subdivisions, methods of determining a horoscope, and the influence of the zodiac on human life.

MANSIONS OF THE MOON
This expression refers to a series of twenty-eight divisions of the Moon's travel through one complete circuit of 360 degrees, each Mansion representing one day's average travel of the Moon, beginning apparently at the point of the Spring Equinox, or zero degree Aries.

MARBOD
(1035-1123) Bishop of Rennes and poet. Author of *Libri Lapidum,* Books of Stones, dealing with the properties of gems and their medical values. Marbod also wrote *De Fato et Genesi,* On Fate and Birth, in which he inveighs against genethlialogy and against the predictions made from the constellations.

MARC ANTONY
It is said that Mark Antony never traveled without an astrologer recommended to him by Cleopatra.

MARCO POLO
(c. 1254-1324) Marco Polo, the famous Italian traveler, bore testimony to the accurate predictions of the Chinese astrologers.

MARS
The planet Mars takes 687 days to encircle the Sun, as astrologers have long known.

MARTIAN
This term is applied to a person under the influence of, or ruled by, a strongly placed Mars.

MATERNUS, IULIUS FIRMICUS

A Roman writer who flourished in the fourth century A.D. He produced a treatise in eight books, entitled *Mathesis*, the subject of which is astrology and magic.

MATHEMATICI

This Latin term designates, like the term Chaldaei, the astrologers and casters of horoscopes who flourished particularly under the Roman Empire.

MATUTINE: MATUTINAL

These terms refer to the Moon, Mercury, and Venus when they appear in the morning. When a star or planet rises before the Sun in the morning, it is called matutine until it reaches its first station, where it becomes Retrograde. The Moon is matutine until it passes its first Dichotomy.

MAYAN CALENDAR

The Mayan calendar was adjusted to planetary motions. This helped the Mayan astrologers to find positions of the stars for a particular day or year.

MAYANS

The Mayans invented the calendar system. Each world corresponded to 1040 years. In the ninth century, when the Mayans had scarcely more than thirty-eight years left before their annihilation, they were seized with an immense fear. A congregation of astronomers-astrologers assembled on the plateaux of Central Mexico to devise a means of escape from the impending cataclysm of the fourth world.

MEAN MOTION

The average motion of any body within a given period. The mean motion of a planet is based on the presumption that it moves in a circle at a uniform rate about the Sun. Actually the planets move in elliptical orbits, in portions of which this motion is accelerated and retarded in ratio to their distance from the gravitational centre.

The Heliocentric mean motions of the planets differ from their geocentric motions.

MEDICAL ASTROLOGY
Through the centuries many physicians have supported the belief in the close affinity between human health and sickness and the planetary system.

The Egyptians, asserted Ptolemy in his *Tetrabiblos*, considered that astrological techniques, in their widest implications, were useful and beneficial in a medical sense, as they determined precautionary measures in treating diseases and remedies for existing illnesses.

MEDICINAL HERBS
According to Pliny the Elder, the Roman encyclopedist and author of the *Natural History*, remedial herbs were associated with the heavenly bodies and with the positions of the planets.

MEDIEVAL DEGREES
In the medieval universities academic degrees were granted in astrological-astronomical studies.

MELANCHTHON
(1497-1560) This German scholar and religious reformer had a decided belief in astrology.

MERCURII
In the nineteenth century, when the interest in astrology was rising, an astrological society was founded in England under the name of "The Mercurii." The founder was a certain professional astrologer named Robert Smith.

MERCURY
This planet, which rules Virgo and Gemini, is regarded by astrologers as lacking in reliability. Ptolemy declared that Mercury assumed the nature of other planets with which he

was associated. There is extant an ancient Homeric *Hymn to Mercury* as a deity.

METHOD OF MAKING PARTICULAR PREDICTIONS

Ptolemy, in his *Tetrabiblos*, expounds the method of making particular predictions with regard to countries and cities. These predictions, he adds, are conditioned by the conjunctions of the sun and moon at eclipse and the movements of the stars at the time.

METONIC CYCLE

The discovery about 432 B.C. by Meton, an Athenian astronomer, of the Moon's period of nineteen years, at the end of which the New Moon occurs on the same day of the year. Upon this he based certain corrections of the lunar calendar. He figured the nineteen-year cycle of 235 lunations to consist of 6,939 days, 16.5 hours. This he divided into 125 full months of thirty days each, and 110 deficient months of twenty-nine days each. The 235 full months, of thirty days each, totalled 7,050 days; hence it became necessary to suppress 110 days or one in sixty-four. Therefore the month which contained the sixty-fourth became a deficient month. As the true lunation period is 6,939 days, 14.5 hours, his calculations showed a deviation of only two hours.

METONIC RETURN

This expression refers to the recurrence of an eclipse on a given degree on the same date some nineteen years later.

MIDHEAVEN

Variant names are *medium coeli*, Southern angle, South point, and cusp of the Tenth House. These terms apply to astrology. Midheaven is sometimes wrongly called the Zenith. More precisely, it is applicable to the South point of the Map, and what it indicates is dependent on the manner of interpretation. Sometimes, too, midheaven is loosely applied to the whole of the Tenth House.

MIDPOINT

This term denotes an unoccupied aspected degree between and equidistant from two other planets, resulting in a symmetrical grouping, sometimes called a planetary picture. Such configurations are regarded as important by some astrologers, although there is some difference of opinion regarding the width of orbs across which there can result a 'transference of light' through the planet which aspects the Midpoint.

MILKY WAY

In old folklore the Milky Way is known as the Road of the Gods. The spirit of a dead person crossed it on the way to its everlasting dwelling-place.

In theosophy the Milky Way is viewed as a vast star-cluster of suns in various degrees of evolutionary growth and the matrix of celestial bodies still unborn.

MILTON, JOHN

(1608-1674) In *Paradise Lost* the English epic poet makes a reference to astrology:

With centric and eccentric scribbled o'er, Cycle and epicycle, orb in orb.

MITHRAIC ASTROLOGY

The cult of Mithra, the Persian Sun-god, dominated all areas of the Roman Empire for more than three centuries. One of the fundamental dogmas of this cult was the belief that the position of the planets, their mutual relationships and energies affect all cosmic phenomena.

MITHRAIC DOCTRINE

According to the doctrine of the Persian cult of Mithra, the cosmos is bound by unchangeable laws and the planets and their inter-relationships affect all earthly phenomena.

MITHRAISM

The ancient Persian cult of Mithra was linked with astrological

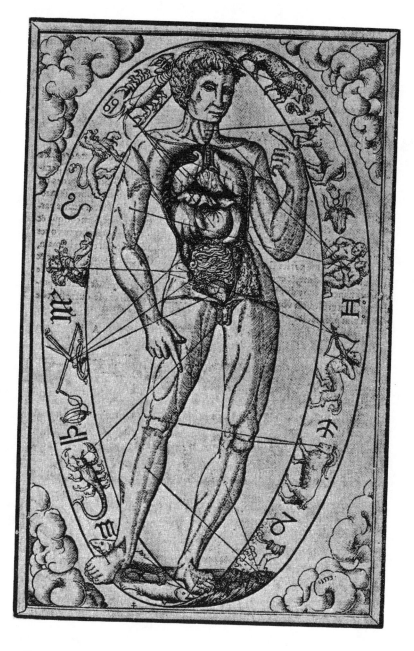

Jollat's "Anatomical Man Surrounded by the Zodiac," showing the influence of the twelve signs.

"An Astrologer Casting a Horoscope." (Robert Fludd, *Utriusque Cosmi Historia*, Oppenheim, 1617.)

concepts, and the planets were associated with certain human attributes or defects. For instance, Mars was related to military prowess, Venus to carnal lust.

MODERATORS
This term was anciently applied by Ptolemy to the Significators: Sun, Moon, Ascendant, Midheaven, Fortuna. It implied that aspects from the Significators moderate or condition the influences of the planets, producing a different 'mode of motion' in the rays reflected. The term is now largely obsolescent.

MODERN ASTROLOGY
In contemporary times the two phases of astrology that are of the greatest interest to the individual seem to be Horary and Natal Astrology. Horary Astrology refers to a figure of the heavens erected for the minute when an issue is in question. Natal Astrology considers the individual from the time of his birth to the end of his life.

MODUS RATIONALIS
This Latin term means *Rational Method.* It is applied to a method of locating the cusps of the intermediate Houses — those which lie between the angular Houses of a Figure — by dividing the Ecliptic by the Equator instead of the semi-arc. Its division into twelve equal parts was accomplished by circles, the cusps located where the circles cut the plane of the Ecliptic. This method has been superseded by the employment of Oblique Ascension under the Poles of the Houses for all but the fourth and tenth cusps.

MOISTURE
Moisture is said to increase when planets are matutine, when the Moon is in her first Quarter, during the winter, and by night.

MONGOL PREDICTION
At the birth of Genghis Khan, the Mongol conqueror, astrologers proclaimed that a divinity had arisen.

MOON

In astrological medicine in the Middle Ages, and even as remotely as Ptolemy, the Moon's position was regarded as a controlling factor in curing sickness.

MOON BOOKS

These were astrological manuals that were current in the eleventh century.

MORGAN, J. P.

The American banker, it is reported, relied on astrological advice in many of his financial undertakings.

MORIN DE VILLEFRANCHE

A seventeenth century French astrologer. In 1661 he published a monumental *Astrologia Gallica*. He was attached to the court of Anne of Austria.

MUNDANE ASPECTS

The aspects formed by planets occupying cusps, whereby it can be said that from the tenth to the twelfth cusps is a Mundane Sextile, though it may be as little as fifty degrees or as much as eighty degrees.

MUNDANE ASTROLOGY

In mundane astrology, the significance of the solar system bodies is as follows:

Sun: executive heads
Moon: the proletariat
Mercury: the intelligentsia
Venus: ambassadors of good will
Mars: military leaders
Jupiter: judiciary
Saturn: state executives
Uranus: air and rail transport
Neptune: social movements
Pluto: organized labor

MUNDANE DIRECTIONS

Mundane Directions or Directions *in mundo* are based solely upon the axial rotation of the earth in relation to the circle of observation whereby planets are carried clockwise through the Houses of the Figure, from east to west, forming aspects to the Ascendant, Midheaven, Sun and Moon. Aspects formed by the opposite or Converse Motion are also employed. The use of spherical trigonometry and of logarithms is necessary for reliable use of this Primary System of Directing. Knowledge of the exact place, hour, and minute is also essential.

MUNDANE PARALLEL

Mundane Parallel or Parallel *in mundo* is a progressed position in which a Significator and a Promittor occupy points on opposite sides and equidistant to any of the four angles of the geocentric Figure: Ascendant, Midheaven. Descendant or Imum Coeli.

MUTABLE SIGNS

Some zodiacal signs are changeable or mutable, while others are fixed or stable.

MUTILATED DEGREES

Certain degrees are said by some astrologers to indicate lameness if rising at birth, or if the Moon or the Ruler of the Ascendant is posited therein.

MUTUAL RECEPTION

This expression refers to two planets mutually posited in each other's essential dignities. For example, with Jupiter in Aries, the Sun's place of exaltation: and the Sun in Cancer, Jupiter's place of exaltation, Sun and Jupiter are said to be in mutual reception. This is accounted a configuration of singular amity and agreement. By some astrologers, the term is confined to the placement of the two planets, each in a house or sign ruled by the other.

NAPOLEON
In his final campaign, Napoleon was informed by his astrologer that he would be defeated at the Battle of Waterloo.

NATIVE
In astrology the term designates either a person born under a particular planet or sign, or the subject of a horoscope or nativity.

NATIVE HOROSCOPY
This is the most popular form of astrological procedure. It involves the genethliacal or natal prognostication of the native.

NATIVITY
Astrologically, the Birth Moment. The instant wherein the native first inhales, thereby beginning a process of blood conditioning that up to that point had been accomplished by the receptivities of another. During the first years of life there ensues a growth of channels of receptivity to cosmic energy which results in a life-pattern of cosmic stimulation. Nativity is also applied to a Figure, or Horoscope, cast for a date, moment, and place of birth, as distinguished from an Electional or Horary Figure.

NAZIS
In 1941 astrologers in Germany were restrained from making

predictions that were inimical to the German political and military situation.

NEBUCHADNEZZAR
In *Daniel* 2.1 the king gave an order to call the magicians and the astrologers to interpret the monarch's dream.

NEBULAE
These are star clusters in which the light of the individual, because of their distance, merges to give the impression of a cloud with a more or less well-defined centre. Great numbers of them are found in the heavens, and when one of them is rising at birth, or is in conjunction with the Moon, it is said to produce blindness or other ocular defects.

The principal nebulae noted in astrology are:
Praesepe, the Hyades, the Pleiades, the Aselli, Aldebaran, Antares.

Ptolemy, referring to the possibility of blindness, mentions the cloudy spot of Cancer, the Pleiades of Taurus, the Arrow-head of Sagittarius, the sting of Scorpio, the parts about the mane of Leo, the urn of Aquarius. The Ascendant or Moon in any of these positions and afflicted by Mars indicates blindness from an accident: afflicted by Saturn, blindness by a natural defect.

NECTANEBUS
An Egyptian king of the fourth century B.C. He was a renowned magician, skilled in divination and the concoction of philtres. By making wax figurines of enemy fleets and of his own forces, he was able in one case, while watching the manoeuvres of the figures in a bowl of Nile water, to forecast victory for his forces and to circumvent imminent disaster by a timely escape.

NERO
The Roman emperor Nero, like Augustus and other emperors of Rome, was in the regular habit of consulting astrologers.

NERO AND THE CHALDEANS
The Roman Emperor Nero proposed to banish all practicing

astrologers, that is, Chaldeans, from Rome. But the Chaldeans announced that their banishment would coincide with the death of the Emperor Himself.

NEWTON, ISAAC
Sir Isaac Newton (1642-1727), the famous mathematician, was encouraged toward the study of astronomy by his reading of astrological treatises.

NIGHT
In Egyptian astrology, the nocturnal hours were unpropitious. With regard to the diurnal hours, some were inauspicious and others favorable.

NIGIDIUS FIGULUS
Roman senator and astrologer who cast the horoscope of the Emperor August and predicted his supreme powers.

NINEVEH
In the nineteenth century cuneiform inscriptions excavated in Nineveh referred to eclipses, phases of the moon, and astrological predictions.

NINTH HOUSE
This term refers to the house of religion, of knowledge: It is governed by the sign of Sagittarius.

NOCTURNAL DIVINITIES
Among the ancient Aztecs of Mexico the night was divided into nine periods. These nine periods were in the nature of divinities, and were called, when the Spaniards came upon the scene, Lords of the Night.

NODES OF THE MOON
Variant names for the nodes are: Ascending and Descending Nodes, the North and South Nodes. Caput Draconis or the Dragon's Head, Cauda Draconis, the Katababazon, or the Dra-

gon's Tail. The Nodes regress about three degrees of arc per day. The Nodes of themselves merely point to places where an incident may happen at a particular time. Events occur because of the time, the place, and the planet, and the Node is often the middle factor in that formula.

NODES OF THE PLANETS
The points at which the orbits of the planets intersect the ecliptic, because of the inclination of their planets to the plane of the earth's orbit. One astrological authority states that a lunation or eclipse on the South Node of a planet tends to release a destructive force of the nature of the planet involved.

NORTHERN SIGNS
This expression denotes the Commanding Signs: Aries to Virgo, pursuing the order of the sign.

NORTH NODE
The North Node of the Moon — The Dragon's Head — is called in Sanskrit Rahu. In Hindu mythology the demon Rahu had a tail of a dragon.

NORTH POINT
This expression denotes the *Imum Coeli* or cusp of the Fourth House. It is placed at the bottom of the Map.

NOSTRADAMUS
(1503-1566). A French physician and astrologer, whose actual name was Michel de Notre-Dame. He is the author of *Centuries*, a series of versified predictions relating to personal and national events, whose occurrence coincided remarkably with his forecasts. At the court of Catherine de Medici he pursued his predictions, including his own death.

NOTABLE NATIVITY
Goethe, the famous German poet (1749-1832) begins his autobiography thus:

On the 28th of August 1749, at midday, as the clock struck twelve, I came into the world, at Frankfort-on-the-Maine. The aspect of the stars was propitious: the sun stood in the sign of the Virgin, and had culminated for the day; Jupiter and Venus looked on with a friendly eye, and Mercury not adversely; the attitude of Saturn and Mars was neutral; the moon alone, just full, exerted all the more as her power of opposition had just reached her planetary hour. She therefore resisted my birth which could not be accomplished until this hour was passed. These auspicious aspects which the astrologers subsequently interpreted very favorably for me may have been the causes of my preservation.

NUMBERS
The Greco-Roman world termed a horoscope 'Babylonian numbers.'

OBLIQUE ASCENSION

As it rises, a star or planet, not on the equator, forms an angle with that part of the equator which is rising at the same time. This is known as its Ascensional difference. This Ascensional difference, added to the rising ascension if it has South declination, and subtracted therefrom if it has North declination, gives its Oblique Ascension.

OBLIQUE DESCENSION

The complement of Oblique Ascension. One hundred-eighty degrees, minus the Oblique Ascension, equals the Oblique Descension.

OCCIDENTAL OR ORIENTAL

These terms have various meanings when differently applied. The Moon is oriental of the Sun when it is increasing in light, from the lunation to the full: occidental of the Sun when decreasing in light. A planet is said to be oriental of the Sun when it rises and sets before the Sun, Planets are said to be stronger when oriental of the Sun and occidental of the Moon. Applied to the Sun, a special significance is involved by the fact when the Sun is setting in one hemisphere it is rising in the other. Therefore the Sun is said to be oriental in Houses 12, 11, 10, 6, 5, or 4; and occidental in the opposite Houses. Thus the oriental Houses are those which have passed the horizon and are culminating toward the meridian: the occidental Houses, those which have passed the meridian and are moving toward the horizon. Some astrologers speak of the Eastern Houses, the entire eastern half of the Figure, as the Oriental Houses: the entire western half, as the Occidental Houses.

OCCULT ARTS
A saying of Heraclitus, the Greek philosopher, who flourished around the sixth century B.C., runs:
The god whose oracle is at Delphi does not speak, does not dissemble. He shows by signs.

OCCULTATION
When a planet or star is hidden or eclipsed by another body, particularly by the Moon, the result is termed an occultation.

OCCURSIONS
This term refers to celestial occurrences such as ingresses, formation of aspects, and conjunctions in astrological phenomena.

OCCURSOR
A term applied by Ptolemy to the planet which moves to produce an occursion. This term is now superseded by Promittor.

OFFICIAL ASTROLOGER
Louis de Wohl, a Hungarian journalist, novelist, and astrologer, became in World War II the sole official astrologer of the British government.

ONE HUNDRED APHORISMS
This is the English title of the Centiloquy, putatively assigned but not conclusively to Ptolemy, author of the *Tetrabiblos*. These maxims deal with horary and elective astrology.

OPINION OF PARACELSUS

Paracelsus (1493-1541), the famous physician and alchemist, wrote of astrology:

Understand, therefore, concerning astrology, that it knows the whole Nature, Wisdom, and Science of the Stars, according as they perfect their own operation in conception and constitute an animal man. But if astrology be fundamentally and properly known, and the nativities of infants be erected rightly according to the mode of the influence, many evils will be avoided which would otherwise be occasioned by the unpropitious constellations.

OPPOSITION

When the zodiacal sign is opposed to Libra, this is called Opposition. This position is regarded as unfavorable.

ORBS

The space within which an aspect is judged to be effective. The term is used to describe the arc between the point at which a platic, or wide aspect, is regarded as strong enough to be operative, and the point of culmination of a partile or exact aspect.

ORIENT

In the Orient, particularly in Japan and Thailand, the practice of astrology is flourishing and its appeal to the public is especially strong.

ORIENTAL ASTROLOGY

The foundation of Oriental astrology rests on the concept that the psychic essence of a person is identical with the fire of the celestial bodies. This astrology postulates a categorical relationship between the human soul and the stars.

ORIGEN

Greek Father of the Church who flourished in the third century A.D. He rejects the practice of casting horoscopes, which would determine the native's life, because such a practice, he felt, destroyed free will.

ORIGIN OF ZODIAC
It has been suggested that the origin of the zodiacal signs stems from the transference of animal deities to the heavens. Probably of Egyptian origin.

ORTIVE DIFFERENCE
This term is sometimes applied to the difference between the primary and secondary distances, when directing the Sun at its rising or setting. It appears to indicate an effort to accommodate the fact of horizontal parallax. In modern times, the term is rarely used.

OXFORD UNIVERSITY
Oxford University, founded in the thirteenth century, regarded astrology, with its co-discipline astronomy, as the most important science. It was also held in the greatest esteem in most medieval universities.

PADMA SAMBHAVA
Hindu scholar called The Precious Guru, who first disseminated astrological knowledge in Tibet. He traveled from India, where he lectured at the Buddhist University of Nalanda, to Tibet. There he founded Lamaism around the year 749 A.D.

PAPACY
Among many pontiffs who employed astrologers were: Pius II, Sixtus IV, Julius II, Leo X.

PAPAL BULL
A Papal Bull, promulgated in 1586, condemned the practice of astrology.

PARACELSUS
(1493-1541) A German physician whose real name was Theophrastus Bombast von Hohenheim. Throughout Europe he practiced medicine and prognostication. He perfected a magic speculum that he used in divination.
He forcefully presented the case of astrology, as follows:

Understand, therefore, concerning Astrology, That it knows the whole nature, wisdom and science of the stars, according as they perfect their own operation in conception and constitute an animal man. But if Astrology be fundamentally and properly known, and the nativities of infants be erected rightly according to the mode of the influence, many evils will be avoided which would otherwise be occasioned by the unpropitious constellations.

PARALLEL
The parallel has the same nature as a conjunction. A mundane parallel is a parallel *in mundo*. It refers to the similarity of relationship between two planets on opposite sides of the Equator. A rapt parallel is a mundane parallel by direction, formed after birth, as the result of the Earth's rotation.

PARKER, GEORGE
(1651-1743) Famous English astrologer. Known for his tables of ephemerides.

PART OF FORTUNE
This is the distance of the moon's position from the sun, plus the degrees of the ascendant.

PARTRIDGE
Jonathan Swift, the eighteenth century satirist, whote a pamphlet in which, under the pen name of Isaac Bickerstaff, he poked fun at a contemporary, an astrologer named John Partridge, who was prolific in publishing many popular almanacs.

PASSIVE
The Sun and the Moon are termed passive, as they take their coloring from the signs in which they are posited, or the planets with which they are in strongest aspect. The Passive Qualities are: Moisture and Dryness.

PENUMBRAL ECLIPSE

Eclipses of the Moon, when the Moon approaches closely enough to the earth's shadow to cause an appreciable diminution of light though it does not directly touch it. These are frequently called appulses. They are not generally classed as eclipses, though from their close resemblance to eclipse conditions they often produce effects similar to those attending an actual eclipse.

PEREGRINE

This term, astrologically, denotes foreign, alien. It refers to a planet posited in a sign where it possesses no essential dignity: where it is neither dignified nor debilitated. It is employed in Horary Astrology, where it is usually reckoned as a debility; in a question of a thief, a peregrine planet in an angle or in the second House is the thief. No planet, however, is reckoned peregrine if it is in mutual reception with another.

PERIODICAL LUNATION

A Figure cast for the Moon's synodic period, when it returns to the exact degree held at birth. It is often employed for monthly forecasts in a way similar to the Solar Revolution for annual forecasts. A true Figure for the Moon's periodical is difficult to construct, because of the Moon's acceleration from hour to hour.

PERIODICALS

In the eighteenth century many periodicals devoted to astrology had a tremendous vogue. Among them was *The Astrologer's Magazine* and *The Conjurer's Magazine*. Early in the nineteenth century *The Struggling Astrologer* appeared under the editorship of Robert Smith, an Englishman. Among his clients, he noted, were the nobility and even royalty. *The Herald of Astrology* was published in England around the same time. It was later on changed to the more popular title of *Zadkiel's Almanac*.

PERIODICITY

The ancient astrologers of Babylon and Chaldea observed that there was a periodicity in the planetary sequences.

PERSISTENT ASTROLOGERS
The Roman emperors Vitellius and Domitian, following their predecessor Augustus, discouraged the practice of astrology. But secretly the astrologers were encouraged in Rome, and persisted with their horoscopes and predictions.

PETER OF ABANO
An Italian philosopher and astrologer who belongs in the thirteenth century. Reputed to have had associations with Satanic forces. Wrote on magic, predictions, and geomancy.

PETRONIUS
Gaius Petronius Arbiter belongs in the first century A.D. In 66 A.D., at the instance of the Emperor Nero, he was forced to commit suicide. He is the author of a novel entitled the *Satyricon*. In the episode called The Banquet of Trimalchio, Petronius makes much of the various dishes served to the guests, each dish representing one of the twelve zodiacal Signs.

PFAFF, JULIUS
Nineteenth century German mathematician who was interested in astrology. In 1816 he published *Astrology*, and also made a complete translation of Ptolemy's *Tetrabiblos*, the supreme source book of astrology that appeared in the second century A.D.

PHILATELY
The popularity of the zodiacal signs as decorative emblems and symbols has become so extensive that the signs have appeared on Israeli postage stamps.

PHILO IUDAEUS
Jewish philosopher of Alexandria, who belongs early in the first century A.D. Of astrology he wrote:
> There is some physical sympathy that makes earthly things depend upon celestial.

Philo displayed an intellectual interest in astrology and interpreted Biblical contexts in astrological terms.

PHOENICIANS
The Phoenicians, Chaldaeans, and Orchinians have familiarity with Leo and the Sun, so that they are simpler, kindly, addicted to astrology, and beyond all men worshippers of the Sun, asserts Ptolemy, in his *Tetrabiblos*.

PISCES
The Fishes. The twelfth southern sign of the zodiac. It represents dissolution of matter followed by resurgence. Esoterically, this sign represents the flood and is the last emanation of the watery trigon. Kabalistically, it signifies the feet of the archetypal man and the mechanical forces of humanity.

PISTIS-SOPHIA
A treatise that is extant in a text of the fifth or sixth century. It postulates the control of all human life by the planets.

PLACIDUS TABLES
These tables were so called because they were established by a seventeenth century Italian astrologer named Placidus de Tito.

PLANETARY AGES OF MAN
The ancients called the planets chronocrators, markers of time. It was presumed that different periods of life were ruled by different planets. The Moon was related to the infant. Mercury referred to the scholar. Venus was attached to the lover. The Sun denoted the citizen. Mars was interested in soldiers. Jupiter implied the judge. Saturn denoted resignation, age.

PLANETARY IMPACTS
The effects of the planets in business, politics, and financial conditions were demonstrated by the popular American astrologer Evangeline Adams.

PLANETARY INFLUENCE
The strongest planetary influence is that of the Sun, which governs the sign of Leo.

PLANETARY MOTIONS

Certain motions are associated with the planets:

Converse — applied to a progressed or directed motion to a point of aspect, in a clockwise direction or opposite to the order of the signs.

Direct — the true motions of the planets in the order of the signs, or counter-clockwise, within the Zodiac. Applied to progressed or directed motion, it is the opposite of converse motion.

Diurnal — a diurnal planet is one that was above the horizon at the time for which the Figure was cast. Such planets are said to be passive.

Rapt — the apparent diurnal motion of the heavens, in consequence of the earth's axial rotation.

Re-direct — applied to the reversal to direct motion following the second station of the retrograde.

Retrograde — the apparent motion in the Zodiac of certain planets, as viewed from the earth during certain parts of the year.

Slow of course — slow in motion. Applied to a planet whose travel in twenty-four hours is less than its mean motion.

Stationary — when a planet appears to have no motion, as when changing from retrograde to direct or the reverse, it is said to be stationary.

Stations, in retrograde — each planet has two stations, or stationary points: 1. the place in its orbit where it becomes stationary before it turns retrograde: 2. when it again becomes stationary preparatory to resuming its direct motion.

Swift in motion — planets that at the moment are moving at a speed in excess of their mean motion are said to be 'swift in motion.'

PLANETARY PATTERN

A symmetrical arrangement of two or more planets or sensitive points around a common axis. A planetary picture as employed in Iranian Astrology represents the inter-activity of two planets, connected through a third planet or sensitive point at or in hard aspect to their midpoint.

PLANETS
The planets are the most important heavenly bodies. They have signs attached to each of their names. The names are as follows: Saturn, Jupiter, Mars, Sun, Venus, Mercury, Moon. The planets and the signs of the zodiac are always present in the heavens but not all are visible. Some lie above and some below the horizon.

PLANETS, CLASSIFICATIONS OF
Planets are classified as:
    barren and fruitful: barren planets are Mars, Saturn, Uranus.
    fruitful: Sun, Moon, Venus, Jupiter, Neptune.
    androgynous: Mercury, which is both dry and moist.
    benefic and malefic: benefic: Venus and Jupiter: malefic: Mars and Saturn.
    cold and hot: Cold – the Moon, Saturn. Hot – Sun, Mars.
    diurnal and nocturnal: nocturnal – the Moon, Venus; diurnal – those which at birth were above the horizon.
    dry and moist: dry – Sun, Mars, Saturn; moist – Mercury, Moon.
    electric and magnetic: electric – Sun, Mars, Jupiter; magnetic – Moon, Mercury, Saturn.
    masculine and feminine:
    masculine – Sun, Mars, Jupiter.
    feminine – Moon, Venus, Neptune.
    morning and evening 'stars'. All the planet terms refer particularly to Mercury and Venus, as morning and evening 'stars', although all the planets become morning and evening stars at some part of the year. Superior and inferior. The major or superior planets are those that have orbits larger than that of the earth and which lie at a greater distance from the Sun. They are: Mars, Jupiter, Saturn, Uranus, Neptune, and Pluto. They are also called the Ponderous or ponderable planets.

The minor or inferior planets are those that have orbits smaller than that of the earth, and which lie closer to the Sun. They are Mercury and Venus.

PLANETS AND METALS
In the Canon's Yeoman's Tale, that appears in Geoffrey Chaucer's (?1340-1400) Canterbury Tales, the Yeoman, an assistant to his master, a Canon-astrologer, assigns metals to their respective planets:

Sol, gold is, Luna's silver, as we see,
Mars iron, and quicksilver's Mercury.
Saturn is lead, and Jupiter tin,
And Venus, copper, by my father's kin.

PLANETS AND ZODIACAL SIGNS
The relation between planets and signs was expounded by the Roman poet Manilius, who belongs in the first century A.D. In his *Astronomica*, a didactic poem on astrology, he writes:

No sign nor planet serves itself alone.
Each blends the other's virtues with its own,
Mixing their force, and interchanged they reign,
Signs planets bound, and planets signs again.

PLANETS IN ACTION
In his *Tetrabiblos* Ptolemy asserts that if Mercury and Venus rule action, they affect music, poetry, dancing, acting.

PLATO
The earliest reference to astrology among the Greeks appears in Plato's dialogue the *Timaeus* 40.

PLATONIC HOROSCOPE
Iulius Firmicus Maternus, who belongs in the fourth century A.D., is the author of an astrological treatise in eight books. In this treatise he erected the horoscope of the Greek philosopher Plato.

PLATO'S ASTROSOPHY
To Plato the stars were "divine and eternal animals, ever abiding." In *The Republic* he describes the music of the spheres, the seven planets, and also the eighth sphere, which is that of the fixed stars.

PLINY THE ELDER
This Roman encyclopedist, who flourished in the first century A.D., was the author of *Historia Naturalis,* in which he discussed the celestial system and proposed an explanation, in astrological terms, of the stations of the superior planets.
Pliny acknowledged the relation between astrology and magic. He refers repeatedly to the common practice of assigning events to particular stars in accordance with horoscopic rules.
Pliny states that the Greek astronomer Hipparchus demonstrated that there is a relationship between the stars and the affairs of men.
Pliny also refers to astrologers in Rome who practiced the casting of horoscopes and offered to predict coming events.

PLOTINUS
Neoplatonic philosopher who belongs in the third century A.D. In one of his treatises he rejects those who cast horoscopes, but again he discusses whether the stars have an influence on human affairs. He accepts the theory that astrological predictions are significant, yet he postulates that human beings have free will.

PLUTO
This planet was discovered in 1930, but its functions and influence are undetermined.

POETIC ASTROLOGY
There are versified characterizations of the zodiacal signs composed, among others, by Addison and Milton, as well as by the ancient Greek poet Aratus and the Roman poet Manilius:

Who works from morn to set of Sun,
And never likes to be outdone?
Whose walk is almost like a run?
  Who? Aries.

Who smiles through life — except when crossed?
Who knows, or thinks he knows, the most?
Who loves good things: baked, boiled, or roast?
  Oh, Taurus.

Who's fond of life and jest and pleasure:
Who vacillates and changes ever?
Who loves attention without measure?
  Why, Gemini.

Who changes like a changeful season:
Holds fast and lets go without reason?
Who is there can give adhesion
  To Cancer?

Soon as the evening shades prevail
The Moon takes up the wondrous tale,
And nightly to the listening Earth
Proclaims the story of her birth.

Who criticizes all she sees:
Yes, e'en would analyze a sneeze?
Who hugs and loves her own disease?
  Humpf, Virgo.

Who praises all his kindred do:
Expects his friends to praise them too —
And cannot see their senseless view?
  Ah, Leo.

Who puts you off with promise gay,
And keeps you waiting half the day?
Who compromises all the way?
  Sweet Libra.

Who keeps an arrow in his bow,
And if you prod, he lets it go?
A fervent friend, a subtle foe —
  Scorpio.

Who loves the dim religious light:
Who always keeps a star in sight?
An optimist both gay and bright —
  Sagittarius.

Who climbs and schemes for wealth and place,
And mourns his brother's fall from grace —
But takes what's due in any case —
  Safe Capricorn.

Who gives to all a helping hand,
But bows his head to no command —
And higher laws doth understand?
Inventor, Genius, Superman —
  Aquarius.

Who prays and serves, and prays some more;
And feeds the beggar at the door —
And weeps o'er love lost long before?
  Poor Pisces.

> — Addison

The Lion flames. There the Sun's course runs hottest.
Empty of grain the arid fields appear
When first the Sun enters.

> — Aratus

But modest Virgo's rays give polished parts,
And fill men's breasts with honesty and arts;
No tricks for gain, nor love of wealth dispense,
But piercing thoughts and winning eloquence.

> — Manilius

  ... Nor dreadful deeds
Might have ensued, nor only Paradise
In this commotion, but the starry cope

Of heaven perhaps, or all the elements
At least had gone to wreck, disturbed and torn
With violence of this conflict, had not seen
The Eternal, to prevent such horrid fray,
Hung forth in heaven his golden scales, yet seen
Betwixt Astraea and the Scorpion sign.
— John Milton, *Paradise Lost*

Bright Scorpio, armed with poisonous tail, prepares
Men's martial minds for violence and for wars.
His venom heats and boils their blood to rage.
And rapine spreads o'er the unlucky age.
— Manilius

Midst golden stars he stands resplendent now,
And thrusts the Scorpion with his bended bow.
— Ovid

And, what was ominous, that very morn
The Sun was entered into Capricorn.
— Dryden

— Pitiless
Siroccos lash the main, when Capricorn
Lodges the Sun and Zeus sends bitter cold
To numb the frozen sailors.
— Aratus

Man's fate and the stars:
Men at some time are masters of their fates;
The fault, dear Brutus, is not in our stars,
But in ourselves, that we are underlings.
— Shakespeare

Westward, and further in the South wind's path,
The Fishes float, one ever uppermost
First hears the boisterous coming of the North.
Both are united by a band.
Their tails point to an angle

140

Filled by a single goodly star,
Called the Conjoiner of the Fishes' Tail.

— Aratus

POETIC CONFIRMATION
Many poets, both ancient and modern, have written on astrology, eulogizing the art and expounding its doctrines. The eminent roster of names includes Homer and Hesiod, Aratus and Manilius, Horace and Vergil, Juvenal, Chaucer, Dante and Milton, Dryden, Byron, Sir Walter Scott and Goethe.

POIMANDRES
A collection of seventeen or eighteen fragments known as the Hermetic Corpus. The first fragment is called Poimandres. This fragment contains astrological matter. The stars are regarded as deities, the Sun being the greatest. The seven planets govern the natural phenomena, while the zodiacal signs too control the human body.

POINT OF LIFE
A progressed point, obtained by advancing zero degrees Aries at the rate of 7 per sign. A planet at this point is presumed to affect the native according to its nature and strength.

POINT OF LOVE
As this represents the position of Venus in a solar figure, and as Venus never has a greater elongation from the Sun than 48 degrees, the Arabian Point can never be in other than the 11th, 12th, 1st or 2nd Houses.

POINT OF THE FATHER
This appears to be the Point of Sudden Advancement except that if Saturn is combust Jupiter is to be taken as the Ascendant in considering the House-position of the Sun.

POLAR ELEVATION
The elevation of the Pole, or the Pole of the Descendant, is relative to the north or south latitude of the place for which a map is erected.

POOR RICHARD
Benjamin Franklin published a series of almanacs under the pseudonym of Richard Saunders or Poor Richard. He borrowed the name from a distinguished astrologer-physician of the preceding century, whose textbook on medical astrology, published in 1677, contained an introduction by the most celebrated of the English astrologers, William Lilly.
In his almanac for 1733 Benjamin Franklin makes the following prediction of the death of his friend and 'fellow student' Titan Leeds:

> He dies by my calculation made at his request, on October 17, 1733, three hours twenty-nine minutes P.M. at the very instant of the conjunction of the Sun and Mercury.

POPES
In the Papacy many pontiffs were learned in astrology: among them Pope Sylvester, John XX, Julius II, Alexander IV, Leo X, Calixtus III.

POPPAEA
Poppaea, the wife of the Emperor Nero, was a profound believer in the court astrologers and their predictions.

POPULAR ASTROLOGY
At the present time the popularity of astrology is so widespread that numerous periodicals are devoted solely to this subject. Furthermore, horoscopes and predictions, in terms of the nativity of a person, are abundantly on the market. Newspapers and television programs also concern themselves with discussion and study of astrological techniques and possibilities.

POPULAR HANDBOOK
In the Middle Ages a widely used manual on astrological techni-

ques was the *De Nativitatibus,* Nativities, composed by the Arab astrologer Mesahala, who belongs in the ninth century A.D.

POPULARITY OF ASTROLOGY
In the United States alone there are more than 2000 periodicals and newspapers that publish regular columns or articles on astrological subjects: advice and guidance in terms of personal horoscopes and prediction based on astrological calculations.

POPULARITY OF HOROSCOPE
The intense interest in the horoscope has led to its popularization in many directions. Horoscopes are now offered while dining. They are printed on menus and on table napkins. The zodiacal signs appear in colorful attractiveness. And there is a general optimistic tone about all the prognostications. The native under each sign is evidently gifted with excellent qualities that will lead to a successful and enriched and happy life. Each sign denotes some positive characteristic, as:

A born leader, or ambitious, or a logical mind, or artistic, or shrewd in business, or optimistic, or forceful, or sympathetic, or intelligent, or pioneer spirit, or vividly imaginative, or trailblazing mind.

PORPHYRY
Ancient Neoplatonic philosopher: died at the beginning of the first century A.D. Prolific writer: author of many treatises on a variety of subjects. Wrote an introduction to *Tetrabiblos,* Ptolemy's astrological treatise.

PORTRAIT OF AN ASTROLOGER
Galeotti Martius was a famous astrologer attached to the court of Louis XI of France. Sir Walter Scott describes Martius thus:

Martius was none of those ascetic, withered, pale professors of mystic learning of those days, who bleared their eyes over the midnight furnace, and macerated their bodies by outmatching the polar bear. He was trained in arms, renowned as a wrestler. His apartment was splendidly furnished, and on a large oaken table lay a variety of mathematical and astrological instruments, all of the most rich materials and curious workmanship. His astrolabe of silver was the gift of the Emperor of Germany and his Jacob's staff of ebony jointed with gold was a mark of esteem from the reigning Pope. In person, the astrologer was a tall, bulky, yet stately man. His features though rather overgrown were dignified and noble, and a Samson might have envied the dark downward sweep of his long descending beard. His dress was a chamber-robe of the richest Genoa velvet, with ample sleeves clasped with frogs of gold and lined with sables. It was fastened round his middle by a broad belt of virgin parchment, round which were represented in crimson characters the signs of the Zodiac.

POSIDONIUS
A Stoic philosopher who belongs in the second century B.C., and who was a noted astrologer.

POSTEL, GUILLAUME
(1510-1581) A French astrologer who traveled widely, delivering lectures in various cities of Europe. He claimed to have received revelations in the stars.

PREDETERMINISM
The Roman historian Tacitus, who belongs in the early decades of the second century A.D., regarded the future life of a person as having been predestined at the moment of birth.

PREDICTION
This is the title of a British periodical devoted to astrological matters and particularly to the erection of horoscopes at the request of readers.

PREDICTIVE ASTROLOGY
The branch of astrology that deals with Directions, the methods by which future influences are ascertained.

PRIEST-ASTROLOGER
In ancient Chaldea the priests were also astrologers, repositories

of all heavenly and secular knowledge. By their astrological calculations they were able to guide the policy of the ruler.

PRIMARY DIRECTIONS
Any method for determining the changing influences of the altered relationship between the cuspal and the planets' places on successive days or years after birth that is based on the diurnal rotation of the earth upon its axis is known as Primary Direction.

PRIMARY SYSTEM
This astrological system is based on the rotation of the earth.

PRINCIPAL PLACES
These are the five places in which the luminaries are said to have the most beneficial effects in a Nativity: the hylegiacal places: the first, eleventh, ninth, and seventh Houses.

PROCESSIONALS
Astrological texts in antiquity had a religious and sacrosanct character. Thus they were borne in the religious processionals during the Egyptian cult ceremonials.

PROFECTIONS
A term used by Ptolemy to indicate the successional rising of the signs, hence of the Sun and other Significators, at the rate of one sign per year.

PROFESSORSHIP
In Salamanca, Spain, a professorship of mathematics and astrology was founded in the thirteenth century. These two disciplines were associated as one unit of the Liberal Arts.

PROGNOSTICATION
I think, even if prognostication be not entirely infallible, at least its possibilities have appeared worthy of the highest regard. — Ptolemy, *Tetrabiblos*.

PROGRESSED HOROSCOPE
A horoscope erected for a date that is as many days after a given birth date as the native's age in years.

PROGRESSIONS
Alterations in the birth chart aiming to show the changing influences that result from motions of the celestial bodies after birth.

PROMITTOR
A planet in which a significator may be 'directed' in order to form an aspect between the 'progressed position' of the significator and the 'birth position' of the promittor, whereby certain events or conditions are promised as concern the significator so directed. The distance the significator must travel to form this aspect is termed the 'arc of direction', to be reduced to time, usually at the rate of one degree for a year.

PROPER MOTION
This expression refers to the motion of a planet in space, as compared with any apparent motion which results from any movement of the earth: either axial rotation, annual revolution, or the motion through space of our entire solar system. The term is also loosely applied to the direct motion of a planet through the signs, in distinction to the diurnal rising and setting caused by the earth's rotation.

PROPHETIC WATERS
It was said that the Emperor Hadrian, who was devoted to astrology, reached the imperial throne of Rome with the help of the prophetic waters of the Castalian spring.

PROROGATOR
This term was used by Ptolemy in connection with a method of direction, effected by proportion of horary times — semi-arcs. The Prorogator is the Apheta or Life Giver, in contrast to the Anareta. By day and in aphetical places the Sun holds the position of Prorogator; by night the Moon.

PTOLEMAEUS
An astrologer to the Roman Emperor Otho, who belongs in the first century A.D.

PTOLEMAIC AND HINDU ASTROLOGY
Astrologically, the Oriental calculations are based on what has been termed a natural zodiac, while that of Occidental people is based on what is called an intellectual zodiac. Approximately 1400 years have passed since these two zodiacs coincided, and there is now a discrepancy of some twenty degrees between the two systems. The Oriental zodiac is therefore about twenty degrees behind the Ptolemaic.

PTOLEMY
Claudius Ptolemaeus of Alexandria belongs in the second century A.D. One of the most eminent ancient astronomers. Author of numerous works on mathematics, geography, and particularly the *Almagest*. He was also interested in astrology in its mathematical aspects.

PYROIS
This term, of Greek origin, refers to Mars and its fiery nature.

QUADRANTINE LUNATION
This term is sometimes applied to the conjunctions, squares, and oppositions of the Sun and the Moon.

QUADRANTS
The four quarters of the celestial figure, representative of the four quarters of the heavens, measured from the cusps of the four angular Houses. The oriental quadrants consist of Houses X to XII inclusive, and IV to VI inclusive. The occidental quadrants, of Houses I to III inclusive, and VIII to IX inclusive. If applied to the zodiac, the oriental quadrants are from Aries to Gemini and from Libra to Sagittarius inclusive, the occidental quadrants consisting of the opposite signs.

QUADRUPEDAL
The four-footed signs: Aries, Taurus, Leo, Sagittarius, Capricorn, all of which represent quadrupeds. Those born when these ascend were said by the ancient astrologers to have the qualities of such animals: as bold as a lion, as lustful as the goat.

QUADRUPLICITY
The zodiacal signs are classified in groups of four called quadruplicities, as follows: cardinal signs: Aries, Cancer, Libra, Capricorn; fixed signs: Taurus, Leo, Scorpio, Aquarius; mutable signs: Gemini, Virgo, Sagittarius, Pisces.

QUALITY OF PREDICTION
The quality of a predicted event, according to Ptolemy in his *Tetrabiblos,* depends on a consideration of the ruling stars.

QUEEN ANNE
(1665-1714) English Queen who was a believer in astrological predictions and took an interest in astrologers.

QUESITED
This term is employed in horary astrology to indicate the person or thing that is the subject of an inquiry.

RADICAL POSITION

This expression refers to a planet's position in a birth horoscope: as distinguished from the transitory or progressed position it occupies at a later date.

RADIX

This term denotes the radical map: the horoscope of birth, the root from which everything is judged. The term is also applied to the radical or birth positions of the planets, as distinguished from their progressed or directed positions. Progressed aspects can never entirely contradict or negate a radical aspect, but must be interpreted only as modifying or mitigating the influences shown in the Radix.

RAMESES II

This Egyptian Pharaoh determined the Cardinal Signs of Aries, Libra, Cancer, and Capricorn.

RAPT PARALLEL

Two bodies, which by rapt motion are carried to a point where they are equidistant from and on opposite sides of the meridian or the horizon, are said to be in Rapt Parallel.

RECEPTION, MUTUAL
This term refers to two planets when they are in each other's sign of exaltation.

RECTIFICATION
The process of verification or correction of the birth moment or ascendant degree of the map, with reference to known events or characteristics relating to the native.

REFORMATION
The Reformation had a pejorative effect on astrological interests. It rejected many traditional beliefs and theories and superstitions, and included astrology among them.

REFRENATION
This term is used in horary astrology when one of two planets applying to an aspect turns retrograde before the aspect is complete. It is taken as an indication that the matter under consideration will not be brought to a successful conclusion.

REGIOMONTANUS
Latin name assumed by Johann Müller (1436-1470), German mathematician, astronomer, and astrologer. Known for his system of astrological division of the Houses.

RELIGION
Astrological interest in antiquity was strengthened and promoted by the almost universal stellar and solar religious cults. With the contemporary breakdown in formal religion, it is felt that astrology has to some extent taken its place and has presumably offered some basis of faith and assurance to the perplexed.

REMOTE PLANET
Before the discovery of Neptune and Uranus, Saturn was regarded, in antiquity, as the most distant planet.

RETROGRADE
This term is applied to an apparent backward motion in the

zodiac of certain planets when decreasing in longitude as viewed from earth.

REVERENCE FOR ASTROLOGY
In ancient China astrology had such a great reputation that an Emperor might be chosen for his knowledge of astronomy-astrology.

RISING SIGN
The sign of the subdivision of the sign which was rising on the eastern horizon at the moment of birth is regarded as exercising a strong influence on the personality and physical appearance of the native.

ROMAN ASTROLOGY
The ancient purpose of astrology was to reduce the motions of the heavenly bodies to mathematical precision. It was concerned with the influence of these bodies on human life.

The temples of Mesopotamia were the earliest to record this view. When the Orient came into contact with Greece, and later Rome came in contact with Hellenic culture, the emphasis on astrology grew until it reached its height in Roman Imperial times. The astrologers who practiced their skill in casting horoscopes were called Chaldaei and Mathematici. A major field of knowledge that was deeply affected by astrology was the practice of medicine.

ROMAN EMPERORS
Among the Roman Emperors who relied on astrological predictions were Augustus, Otho, Vespasian, Domitian, Titus, Marcus Aurelius, Septimius Severus, Alexander Severus. They each had their personal astrologers.

Tiberius himself cast his own horoscopes and the conclusions he drew from them drove him to execute those who threatened his throne. When he tired of an astrologer he had him put to death.

ROMAN HOROSCOPE
Under the Roman Emperor Tiberius, who belongs in the first century A.D., astrologers who cast horoscopes were condemned to death.

ROMAN PREDICTION
A Roman astrologer, on reading the horoscope of the Roman Emperor Caligula (12-41 A.D.), predicted the time of the Emperor's death and also the circumstances.

ROMULUS' HOROSCOPE
In his *Life of Romulus* the Greek biographer Plutarch, explains the horoscope of Romulus, the founder of Rome:
> In the time of Marcus Varro there was a friend of his called Tarratius, a great philosopher and mathematician. It did fall out that Varro gave him this question, to search out what hour and day the nativity of Romulus was. For they say that by the selfsame science one may tell before of things to come, and to happen to a man in his life, knowing certainly the hour of his nativity: and how one may tell also the hour of his nativity.

ROSTER OF ASTROLOGERS
Among famous Jewish astrologers were many who flourished in the Middle Ages. Included among them were:
> Solomon ibn Gabirol, Andruzagar ben Zadi Farouk, Jacob ibn Tarik, Abraham ben Hiyya, Judah Ha-Levi, Abraham ibn Said, Isaac Arama, Solomon ben Adnet.

ROVING ASTROLOGERS
During the Roman Empire Chaldean astrologers roamed the highways of Italy in quest of clients.

ROYAL ADVISERS
The astrologers Angelo Catto and d'Almonsor were treated royally at the court of Louis XI of France (1423-1483).

ROYAL SCIENCE
Astrology in antiquity was regarded as an art or science associated with royal status. In Babylonia astrologers were attached to the royal courts. In Imperial Rome, similarly, the Emperors had their own professional astrologers. In the Middle Ages, also, the Pontiffs consulted their papal astrologers.
Queen Elizabeth I of England had as her court astrologer the famous occultist and mathematician Dr. John Dee.

RUDOLPHINE TABLES
Johannes Kepler (1571-1630), one of the most eminent astronomers, published Tycho Brahe's astronomical observations in the *Rudolphine Tables*. The Tables were so called because Brahe was under the patronage of Rodolph II of Denmark.

RULING PLANET
When a planet is in a zodiacal sign of which it is the ruler, it is said to be on its throne.

RUMINANT SIGNS
This expression refers to Aries, Taurus, Capricorn.

SABIANS
The ancient sect of Sabians, established in Harran, displayed a deep interest in all phases of astrology and the conjunctions and oppositions, the stations of the planets, the influence of the zodiacal signs on the native.

SACERDOTAL ASTROLOGY
In ancient times, the astrologer and the priest were often united in the same person. The astrologers assumed a sacred prestige that linked them with the divine celestial bodies. The priests of the Persian cult of Mithra were similarly devotees of astrology, and their dedication was to the stars: that is, the deities, benign or malefic controllers of all earthly phenomena, including mankind.

SACRED ASTROLOGICAL CALENDAR
The astrological calendar of the Aztecs was originated by the god Quetzalcoatl:

The gods thought it well that the people should have some means of writing by which they might direct themselves, and two of their number, Oxomoco and Cipactonal, who dwelt in a cave in Cuernavaca, especially considered the matter. Cipactonal thought that her descendant Quetzalcoatl should be consulted, and she called him into counsel. He, too, thought the idea of the calendar good, and the three addressed themselves to the task of making the *Tonalamatl*, or Book of Fate. To Cipactonal was given the privilege of choosing and writing the first sign, or day-symbol of the calendar. She painted the *Cipactli* or dragon animal, and called the sign *Ce Cipactli* ('one *Cipactli*'). Oxomoco then wrote *Om Acatl* ('two canes') and Quetzalcoatl 'three houses' and so on, until the thirteen signs were completed.

SAGITTARIUS
The Archer. The ninth, southern sign of the zodiac. It represents the corporeal and the spiritual elements constituting man. Esoterically, it represents the organizing power of the mind as well as retribution. Kabalistically it signifies the thighs of the old man of the heavens and represents stability and authority.

SALAMANCA
In Salamanca, Spain, a chair of mathematics and astrology was established in the thirteenth century.

SAMBACH, JOHANN GEORG
German astrologer who belongs in the seventeenth century. Author of *Astrologer's Mirror,* which appeared in Nuremberg in 1680.

SARGON
In the reign of Sargon of Accad, king of Babylonia, who belongs in the fourth millennium B.C., every temple had a library devoted to astrological studies and calculations.

SAROS
A Chaldean and Babylonian interpretation of a cycle of sixty days as sixty years. The interpretation also denotes sixty sixties or 3,600. Also a lunar cycle of 6,585,320 days — 23 lunations.

SATURN

To this planet have been assigned a number of different functions. Of all the planets, he is the most powerful. He is also involved in occultism.

SATURN AND MARS

Saturn, allied with Mars, declares Ptolemy, in honorable positions, makes subjects who are harsh, pitiless, disdainful, unbending, grasping, tyrannical, malignant, belligerent, boastful, unjust, haters.

SCIENCE OF NATIVITIES

Ptolemy, in his *Tetrabiblos,* expounds in detail the subdivisions of the science of nativities.

SCIENTIFIC TESTIMONY

Among notable names of men skilled in various disciplines and equally knowledgeable in astrology are: Hippocrates, the father of medical science: Vitruvius, author of a Latin treatise on architecture: Placidus, a mathematician: Giordano Bruno, martyred for science: Jerome Cardan, mathematician: Copernicus, Galileo, Gassendi, Tycho Brahe, Regiomontanus, Kepler, Huygens, all astronomers: Roger Bacon, the Benedictine monk: Francis Bacon the philosopher: Napier, inventor of logarithms: Flamstead, founder of Greenwich Observatory: Elias Ashmole of Oxford.

SCORPIO

The Scorpion. The eighth, southern sign of the zodiac. It represents the human span of life. Esoterically, the Scorpion signifies death and deceit, the allegorical serpent that tempted Eve.

Kabalistically, it represents the procreative system of humanity.

SCOT, MICHAEL

(c. 1175-1234) Noted Scottish astrologer and occultist. He was attached to the court of Frederick II, King of Sicily and Naples. Apart from many translations into Latin from Greek and Arab writers, he was particularly adept in judicial astrology. There is a reference to him in Dante.

SECONDARY PROGRESSIONS
Zodiacal aspects formed by the orbital motions of the planets on successive days after birth, each day accounted the equivalent of one year of life. Aspects are calculated to the birth positions of the luminaries, planets, and angles, and mutual aspects are formed between the progressed planets.

SELEUCUS, BARBILLUS
Two astrologers who were attached to the court of the Roman emperor Vespasian (9-79 A.D.).

SENECA
This Roman Stoic philosopher, who belongs in the first century A.D., stated that the stars are portents of future events, just as a person's star at nativity determines his life.

SENECA'S CONTENTION
Seneca, the Roman Stoic philosopher and dramatist, author of *Natural Questions* and other works, believed that whatever occurs is a symbol of a future event.

SENSES, SIGNIFICATORS OF
The significators of the five physical senses are:
    Mercury: sight.
    Venus: touch.
    Mars: taste.
    Jupiter: smell.
    Saturn: hearing.

SEPHARIAL
This was the pseudonym of Walter Old, a nineteenth century astrologer who had great popularity in England. For a brief pe-

riod he published a periodical entitled *Fate and Fortune*.

SEVEN PLANETS
In antiquity the planets were arranged with relation to their distance from the earth, as follows:
Moon
Mercury
Venus
Sun
Mars
Jupiter
Saturn
Each of these planets is a Ruler of a zodiacal sign or of more than one sign.

SEVEN SUNS
According to Hindu astrology, The Seven Suns of the Dragon of Wisdom govern the destiny of the universe.

SEVENTH HOUSE
This term refers to the house of love and marriage. It is governed by the sign of Scorpio.

SEVERUS
This Roman emperor (146-211 A.D.), who was a skilled astrologer, discovered that he could crush a revolt that had broken out in the colony of Britain. He also discovered through astrological calculations that after he had put down the uprising he himself would never return to Rome. He died at Eboracum, which is now York.
His wife Julia was also an adept in astrology.

SEXUALITY
Astrology is closely associated with sexuality and involves the position of Venus in its signs, aspects, and relation to man, and the Fifth House and the Seventh House, which determine sentimental and emotional contacts.

159

SHAKESPEAREAN ALLUSION
Many illustrations, references, and expositions dealing with astrology occur in the Shakespearean plays. In one drama a player expounds: It is impossible that anything should be as I would have it; for I was born, sir, when the Crab was ascending; and all my affairs go backwards.

SHAKESPEARE'S INTEREST
Throughout the Shakespearean corpus of dramas there occur not only occasional references to astrological concepts, but dialogues as well that indicate Shakespeare's knowledge of the subject. Such allusions and conversations appear in *King Lear, Antony and Cleopatra, Twelfth Night, All's Well that Ends Well, Much Ado about Nothing.*

SHELLEY, PERCY B.
(1792-1822) The poet Shelley's horoscope showed the constellation Argo in the eighth House, which is the House of death. Argo is associated with ships and the sea. The poet died by drowning.

SIBLY, EBENEZER
An eighteenth century English surgeon and astrologer. He was the author of *The Celestial Science of Astrology,* published in 1790.

SIGNIFICATOR
A planet may be taken as a significator of a person or an event, or of affairs ruled by a House. Its strength by virtue of its Sign and House position and its relationship by aspects are then consulted in arriving at a judgment concerning a desired condition. In general the strongest planet in the Figure, usually the ruler of the Ascendant, is taken as the Significator of the native. Similarly the Ruler of the Sign on the cusp of the Second House is taken as the Significator of wealth, of the

Seventh House of the partner, of the Eighth of the partner's wealth, and so on.

SINISTER
A left-handed aspect – not, however, with reference to the proper motion of the aspecting body, but to its apparent motion.

SIXTH HOUSE
This term refers to health. It is governed by the sign of Virgo.

SIXTUS IV
This fifteenth century Pope took a deep interest in astrology. He determined important dates by making use of planetary hours.

SOLAR EQUILIBRIUM
A term used recently by astrologers with reference to the solar Figure: one cast for sunrise on a given day, but with Houses of uniformly thirty degrees each.

SOLAR REVOLUTION
A horoscopical figure erected for the moment in any year when the Sun has reached the exact Longitude it occupies in the Radix. From this figure and from aspects of Radical planets to significators – Sun, Moon, Ascendant, and Midheaven degrees – in the Solar Revolution map predictions are made covering the ensuing year.

SOLAR SYMBOL
The circle represents eternity, while the dot symbolizes the appearance of primary power.

SOLAR SYSTEM BODIES, INFLUENCE OF
In external affairs, the solar system bodies exercise influence as follows:

Sun: leaders in authority.
Moon: public life.
Mercury: business.

Venus: social activities.
Mars: weapons of war.
Jupiter: material wealth.
Saturn: poverty, decay.
Uranus: power, authority.
Neptune: popular movements.
Pluto: idealistic organizations.

SOLINUS
A Latin writer who belongs possibly in the fourth century A.D. In his work on a universal geography, he refers to the horoscope of the city of Rome and the details of its first founding.

SONS OF HORUS
In Egyptian astrology, these were the jackal head, the hawk head, the human head, the dog head: all equated with the four fixed signs of the zodiac.

SOUTH LATITUDES
The latitudes south of the celestial equator. In using the Table of Houses, for South Latitudes, signs are changed to their opposites: for instance, Aries becomes Libra.

SPAIN
After the conquest of Spain by the Moors, the study of astrology took on an intense impetus. Among the notable names was Alonzo of Castile, whose Alonzine Tables were finally arranged by Jewish and Christian scholars.

SPECULUM
A table appended to a horoscope, comprising its astronomical elements: the planet's latitude, declination, Right Ascension, Ascensional Difference, Pole and Semi-arc. It is employed in the practice of directing by Primary Directions as taught by Ptolemy.

SPHERE OF APULEIUS
A medieval chart used to determine, in the case of sickness,

whether the illness would be fatal or the person would recover.

STARRY INFLUENCE
Some astrologers credit the stars with an influence of their own, when in conjunction and parallel with a planet, either at birth or in transit. A star of the first magnitude on the Ascendant or Midheaven at birth is said to indicate that the native will become illustrious within his sphere life. The two large stars, Aldebaran and Antares, which are in the ninth degree of Gemini and Sagittarius respectively, when directed to the angles of the horoscope, are said to produce periods of severe stress. They are considered more powerful when on the angles.

STATE AND FAMILY
In ancient China astrology was regarded as a state matter. Official astrologers expounded the conditions, in astrological terms, by which both the state and then the individual family were to be ruled.

STATIONS
Stations are those points in the orbit of a planet where it becomes either retrograde or direct. So termed because it remains stationary there for a few days before it changes its course. The first station is where it becomes retrograde: the second station, where it abandons retrograde and resumes direct motion. From these stations orientality is reckoned. From apogee to the first station it is matutine, because it rises in the morning before the Sun, hence it is in the first degree of orientality. From the first station to perigee, the lowest apsis, it is vespertine, because it rises in the evening before Sunset, hence it is the first degree of orientality.

STATIONS OF THE MOON
The Moon is never retrograde, but in a different sense her first and second dichotomies are often loosely termed her first and second stations.

STATUE TO ASTROLOGER
The skill of the ancient Chaldean astrologer Berosus was so great that at his death a statue was set up to commemorate him. The statue was made to show a golden tongue, symbolic of the veracity of Berosus' predictions.

STELLAR DIVINITIES
The Greeks and the Babylonians conceived the planets as divinities. Aristotle also refers to an ancient Greek belief in the divinity of the stars.

STELLAR POSITIONS
In ancient Egypt, as early as the thirteenth century B.C., the Egyptians had marked out the positions of the stars.

STELLAR RECORDS
According to Cicero, the Roman philosopher, in his *De Divinatione,* On divination, the Chaldeans had records of the stars covering a period of 370,000 years. Cicero adds that the Babylonians over a period of many thousands of years kept the nativities of all children who were born among them.

STERNE, LAURENCE
In his novel *The Life and Opinions of Tristram Shandy,* Laurence Sterne, the English novelist who belongs in the eighteenth century, pokes fun at astrology and the casting of horoscopes.

STOICS
The ancient Greek philosophers, the Stoics, and especially Posidonius, were responsible for the introduction of astrology into Greece.

SUBLIME SCIENCE
Abraham ibn Ezra (1092-1167), the famous Jewish philosopher, called astrology The Sublime Science. He is the subject of Robert Browning's poem 'Rabbi Ben Ezra.'

SUCCEDENT HOUSES
Those Houses which follow the angular Houses: 2, 5, 8 and 11.

SUMERIANS
The Sumerians and Babylonians believed that the will of the gods in respect to man and his affairs could be learned by watching the motions of the stars and planets, and that skilled star-gazers could obtain from the motions and varying aspects of the heavenly bodies indications of future calamity and prosperity.

SUN AND MOON
The Sun and the Moon have each one house only. The Sun resides in Leo. The Moon resides in Cancer.
In the Mithraic mystery cult the two luminaries were the object of worship.

SUN AS DEITY
In antiquity, the worship of the Sun as a divinity was prevalent, particularly in the Near East. Mithra, the Phrygian deity, was *Sol Invictus,* the Unconquerable Sun. Ra in Egypt was the Sun-god. Shamash too was the Near East Sun-god. Helios was the Greek Sun-god. Phoebus Apollo was the Roman deity of the Sun. Julian the Apostate wrote a Hymn to the divine Sun. Among the Aztecs, the Mayans, and the Incas, the Sun was similarly glorified as a divinity.
Correspondingly, the Moon was worshipped in classic antiquity as the Moon goddess, Selene, Diana.

SUNDAY
Astrologically, birth on Sunday is a sign of good fortune: particularly on Palm Sunday, and especially in the case of a girl. She is destined to make a rich and happy marriage.

SUPERIOR PLANETS
Those planets which lie outside of the earth's orbit.

SWIFT, JONATHAN
(1667-1745) Dean Swift wrote a satire on astrological predic-

tions. It is entitled *Predictions for the Year 1708, by Isaac Bickerstaff*. It was directed in particular against an almanac maker named Partridge.

SWIFT IN MOTION
This expression is applied to a planet whose travel in twenty-four hours exceeds its mean motion.

SWITZERLAND
During World War I astrological societies were established in Switzerland, notably in Zürich.

SYMBOLISM OF THE ZODIAC
The four signs of the zodiac that represent Ezekiel's vision of the living creatures are: Taurus, Leo, Aquarius, and Scorpio.

SYNESIUS
Bishop of Ptolemais in Egypt. Neoplatonic philosopher who belongs in the fifth century A.D. As a mathematician and an astronomer, Synesius had a strong belief in astrology, alchemy, and the occult arts.
He supported the claims of astrology as being serviceable to the study of theology.

SYNTHESIS
The art of blending together separate influences in a nativity and deducing a summary thereof. The ability to synthesize a nativity is the mark of an experienced astrologer.

SYRIAN PRIESTS
In antiquity the priest of the Syrian cults followed Chaldean astrological techniques whereby their theology assumed a scientific basis.

SYZGY
This term, of Greek origin, means *a yoking together*. It is often loosely applied to any conjunction or opposition: particularly of a planet with the Sun, and close to the ecliptic whereby

the earth and the two bodies are in a straight line. In its use in connection with the calculations of Tide Tables it applies to the conjunctions and oppositions of Sun and Moon near the Node.

The fraudulent astrologer receives a client

TABLES OF HOUSES
Tables showing the degrees of the signs which occupy the cusps of the several Houses in different latitudes for every degree of Right Ascension, or for every four minutes of Sidereal Time.

TABLET OF CAMBYSES
An astrological chart belonging in the sixth century B.C. Cambyses was a king of Persia.

TACITUS
Tacitus, the Roman historian who belongs in the second century A.D., considered that Saturn had the greatest power over human affairs.

TAROT
Tarot cards, seventy-eight in number, are often used by Gypsies in fortune-telling. They have also been used by professional astrologers as divinatory aids.

TARRUTIUS
A famous astrologer who flourished in the first century B.C. He had a friend, Marcus Terentius Varro, who requested the

astrologer to calculate the horoscope of Romulus, the mythical founder of Rome.

TAURUS
The Bull. The second, northern sign of the zodiac. Taurus is equated with the procreative function. In occultism its genus is symbolized as Aphrodite. Kabalistically, the sign represents the ears, neck, and throat of the grand old man of the skies. Thus Taurus is the silent, patient principle of humanity.

TEMPERAMENT AND THE HEAVENLY BODIES
One would find the nature of the inhabitants of Asia conform with the temperaments governed by Venus and Saturn in oriental aspects. For they revere the star of Venus under the name of Isis, and that of Saturn as Mithra Helios. Most of them, too, divine future events. — Ptolemy, *Tetrabiblos.*

TENTH HOUSE
This term refers to ambition, prestige. It is governed by the sign of Capricorn.

TERMINAL HOUSES
The fourth, eighth, twelfth Houses, corresponding to the signs of the Watery Triplicity. So called because they govern the termination of three occult or mysterious phases of life: the fourth, the end of physical man: the eighth, the liberation of the soul: the twelfth, the liberation of the hopes to which the native secretly aspires.

TERMS OF THE PLANETS
These terms comprise a system of subrulerships of portions of a sign by different planets, whereby the nature of a planet posited in a sign is altered to that of the planet in whose term it happens to be posited.

TESTIMONY
A partial judgment based on the influence of a certain planet

as conditioned by sign and House, strength of position and aspects, or of a certain configuration of planets in a Figure. The synthesis of several testimonies constitutes a judgment. The term, as used by Ptolemy, is approximately synonymous with Argument.

TESTIMONY ON ASTROLOGY

Many famous personalities, both in antiquity and in modern times, have testified to their interest, and often to their belief, in astrological phenomena. To Dante, the author of the Divine Comedy, astrology was "the noblest of the sciences." He declares:

> I saw
> The sign that follows Taurus, and was in it.
> ...O light impregnated
> With mighty virtues, from which I acknowledge
> All my genius, whatsoe'er it be.

John Ruskin stated:
> The greatness or the smallness of a man is, in the most conclusive sense, determined for him at his birth.

Tycho Brahe was quite categorical in asserting:
> The stars rule the lot of Man.

Johannes Kepler the astronomer:
> An unfailing experience of mundane events in harmony with the changes occurring in the heavens has instructed and compelled my unwilling belief.

Sir Walter Scott:
> Do not Christians and Heathens, Jews and Gentiles, poets and philosophers, unite in allowing the starry influences?

Francis Bacon:
> The natures and dispositions of men are, not without truth, distinguished from the predominances of the planets.

St. Thomas Aquinas:
> The celestial bodies are the cause of all that takes place in the sublunar world.

John Milton:

Knowledge by favor sent
Down from the empyrean, to forewarn
Us timely.

Hippocrates:
A physician without a knowledge of astrology has no right to call himself a physician.

Benjamin Franklin predicted a future event by astrological calculation:
by my calculation... on October 17th ... at the instant of the conjunction of Sun and Mercury.

Theodore Roosevelt:
I always keep my weather-eye on the opposition of my Seventh House Moon to my First House Mars.

Goethe:
These auspicious aspects, which the astrologers subsequently interpreted for me, may have been the causes of my preservation.

Shakespeare:
The stars above govern our conditions.

TETRABIBLOS
This term, of Greek origin, means *four books*. It is the title of the oldest record of the astrological system of the ancients which has survived. It dates from about 132-160 A.D. Here the author, Claudius Ptolemaeus, says that it was compiled from 'ancient' sources.

TETRAGONUM
A line drawn from Aries, Cancer, Libra, Capricorn forms a tetragonum or quartile. This figure is regarded as unfavorable.

TEXTS
Cuneiform texts, many still extant, formed a kind of library in the temples of Babylon. These texts contain astrological references and predictions.

THE FRUITS OF HIS BOOK
This is variant title for the *Centiloquy*, the collection of one hundred maxims on horary astrology attributed to Ptolemy, author of the *Tetrabiblos*.

THE GREAT KHAN
When Genghis Khan, the Mongol conqueror, was a child, it was predicted by astrologers that he would eventually become the Khan of all Tartary.

THE HEAVENS AND THE EARTH
St. Thomas Aquinas (1225-1274,) famous Italian scholastic philosopher, known as the Doctor Angelicus and Prince of Scholastics, declared that the celestial bodies are the cause of all that takes place in the sublunar world.

THE HOROSCOPE
This is the title of a ballet produced in London in 1938, based on astrological motifs.

THEOGENES
A Greek astrologer, who belongs in the first century B.C. Before Augustus Caesar became the first Roman Emperor, Theogenes predicted his imperial ascent.

THE SECRET OF SECRETS
This is a treatise containing astrological material. The work, which was popular in the Middle Ages, was wrongly attributed to Aristotle.

THE SOUL OF ASTROLOGY
This is the title of an astrological treatise. It was published in 1649 by Dr. William Salmon. He was also editor of a number of works on alchemy.

THE SPARKLING ONE
This expression was assigned by the ancient Greeks to the planet Mercury.

THIRD HOUSE
This term refers to the house of possessions. It is governed by the sign of Taurus.

THOTH
Hermes Trismegistus, The Thrice Greatest, was, in Egyptian mythology, equated with the god Thoth, the inventor of astrology.

THRASYLLUS OF ALEXANDRIA
(died 36 A.D.) A noted astrologer who taught the art to the Roman Emperor Tiberius. Thrasyllus is the author of treatises on astrology.

THREE WISE MEN
The Three Wise Men of the East, in the Biblical context, were, at the beginning of the Christian era, conceived as Saturn, Jupiter, and Mars.

THRONE
A planet is said to be on its throne when in a sign of which it is the Ruler. In a more ancient usage it was applied to a planet posited in that part a sign wherein it had more than one Dignity.

THUNDERSTORMS
The Roman Emperor Tiberius believed in the prognostication of weather conditions, particularly thunderstorms. He had great faith too in Chaldean astrology. He himself had been the pupil of the astrologer Thrasyllus.

TIBET
In Tibet the lama-astrologer was consulted by the Tibetans. The prognosticator compared the planetary positions of the native's birth-moment with the day of the consultation. From this he diagnosed the success or failure of a project.
In the case of marriage, the astrologer compared the horoscopes

of the betrothed couple and if he saw therein no satisfactory affinities, the couple would be advised not to marry.

TIBETAN ASTROLOGER
Padma Sambhava, Tibetan astrologer, founded the religious-philosophical system of Lamaism in the middle of the eighth century A.D.

TOSCANELLI, PAOLO
Italian astrologer who belongs in the fifteenth century. He was attached to the court of Cosimo de Medici.

TRANSITOR
A slow-moving major planet whose lingering aspect to a birth planet produces a displacement of equilibrium, which is then activated by an additional aspect from a Culminator, a faster-moving body such as the Sun or Moon, to the same or another planet, thereby precipitating the externalization.

TRANSLATION OF LIGHT
The conveyance of influence which occurs when a transiting planet is found to be applying to an aspect of another, in which case some of the influence of the first aspected planet is imparted to the second aspected planet by a translation of light.

TRANSMUTATION
The advantageous utilization, on the part of a controlled and developed character, of an astrological influence which otherwise might exert a destructive and disruptive force. The term is borrowed from alchemy.

TREATISE ON ASTROLOGY
A treatise on predicting the future by the stars was ascribed to the putative authorship of Apollonius of Tyana, Greek philosopher and magician, who flourished in the first century A.D.

TRIGON
This term is applied to the three signs of the same triplicity.

TRIGRAMS
Eight trigrams which combine to form sixty-four hexagrams or Kuas are the basis of the Chinese technique of divination. The sixty-four Kuas of the *I Ching* express the complete range of situations in which man may find himself.

TRIMORION
An aspect in mundo which embraces three Houses, hence a mundane square, but which in some instances may actually extend to as much as 120 degrees. Hence in Primary Directions it was sometimes called the killing arc, since 120 years were considered the natural limit of life.

TRINE
This is a line drawn from the signs of the zodiac Aries, Sagittarius, Leo and then back to Aries. A triangle is thus formed which is called trine. Trine is a favorable figure.

TRINITIES
A classification of the twelve signs into four groups, representing the four seasons, is called the Trinities:

Intellectual	Maternal	Reproductive	Serving
(Spring)	(Summer)	(Autumn)	(Winter)
1. Aries	4. Cancer	7. Libra	10. Capricorn
2. Taurus	5. Leo	8. Scorpio	11. Aquarius
3. Gemini	6. Virgo	9. Sagittarius	12. Pisces

TRIPLICITY
The zodiacal signs are classified in groups of three, called triplicities, as follows:
Fire signs: Aries, Leo, Sagittarius
Air signs: Gemini, Libra, Aquarius
Earth signs: Taurus, Virgo, Capricorn
Water signs: Cancer, Scorpio, Pisces

TRUTINE
A term employed by Hermes in the process of rectification.

TURKISH PREDICTION
Othman I, Turkish ruler, had an official astrologer attached to his court who predicted the rise of the Ottoman Empire.

TWELFTH HOUSE
This term refers to enemies. It is governed by the sign of Pisces.

TWO CALENDARS
In ancient Egypt there were two calendars in use. One calendar consisted of 365 days: the other, by which sacred festivals were reckoned, of 365¼ days.

TWO METHODS
Among the astrologers of ancient Babylon there was in use a spherical method of calculating, and a cosmic method in terms of the stars.

TYPES OF ASTROLOGY
Natural astrology is that branch of astrology that predicts the movements of the celestial system.
Horary astrology is associated with the casting of horoscopes.
Judicial astrology expounds the celestial bodies in relation to men's lives on this planet.
Mundane astrology refers to the affairs of the state, of an entire nation, or of the global system itself.
Meteorological astrology deals with the forecasts of weather conditions.

TYPOCOSMY
This term was assigned to a kind of astro-symbolical system devised by Karl Ernst Krafft, a Swiss astrologer who reputedly was Hitler's official prognosticator with regard to military and political policies.

UMBRAL ECLIPSE
This term is applied to an eclipse of the Moon, when the Moon definitely enters the earth's shadow. If the Moon is completely immersed in the earth's shadow a total eclipse results: otherwise, a partial eclipse. Applied to an eclipse of the Sun the term does not include a partial eclipse, but only those in which the Moon's disc is fully contained within that of the Sun, either total annular, or annular-total.

UNFORTUNATE SIGNS
The negative signs: Taurus, Cancer, Virgo, Scorpio, Capricorn, Aquarius.

UNIVERSAL CONFLAGRATION
Seneca, the Roman Stoic philosopher (c. 4 B.C. - 65 A.D.,) declared that when all the stars were in conjunction in the sign of Cancer, a universal conflagration would occur.

UNIVERSAL TESTIMONY
Sir Walter Scott, the novelist and poet, asked:
Do not Christians and Heathens, Jews and Gentiles, poets and philosophers unite in allowing the starry influences?

URANIA

This is the title of an English astrological periodical that appeared in the late nineteenth century.

URANIAN

This term is applied to a person of erratic and independent nature, with original and unorthodox ideas and viewpoints, due to a strong Uranus birth receptivity.

URANUS

This planet was discovered by the English astronomer Sir William Herschel in 1781 and was originally called after him. The characteristics and influence of Uranus, however, have not been decisively determined by professional astrologers.

VALENS
Roman Emperor who flourished in the fourth century A.D. He had a court astrologer named Heliodorus, who predicted the future from observation of the stars. He also cast horoscopes.

VALIDITY OF ASTROLOGY
According to Ptolemy in his *Tetrabiblos*, the validity of astrological predictions should be measured by the frequency not of inaccuracies and errors, but of true prognostications and interpretations.

VARIANT NAMES
In ancient Rome astrologers, casters of horoscopes and similar prognostications were termed astrologi, mathematici, genethliaci, Chaldaei, Babylonii.

VERSIFIED ASTROLOGY
Samuel Butler (1612-1680), English satirical poet. Author of a mock-heroic poem entitled *Hudibras*. This satirizes, among other themes, the passion for astrological studies. One of the characters, Hudibras himself, finds:
  A Moon-dial, with Napier's bones,

179

And several constellation stones,
Engraved in planetary hours,
That over mortals had strange powers

To make 'em thrive in law or trade,
And stab or poison to evade;
In wit or wisdom to improve,
And be victorious in love.

VERSE PROGNOSTICATION
There is extant a collection of versified prognostications. The authorship is in dispute, but the date of the text is assigned to the third century A.D.

VESPERTINE
This term is applied to a planet which sets in the West after the Sun. The reverse is Matutine.

VETTIUS, VALENS
A writer on astrological subjects who belongs in the second century A.D.

VIA COMBUSTA
The combust path. As employed by the ancients this doubtless referred to a cluster of fixed stars in the early degrees of the constellation Scorpio. A birth Moon in that arc was considered to be as afflicted as if it were in an eclipse condition — at or near one of the Nodes. If so, the description would have to be revised by one degree every seventy years, to compensate for the Precessional arc. This would probably place the Via Combusta in the region occupied by Antares and opposed by Aldebaran, an arc now centering around ten degrees Sagittarius. A birth planet or birth Moon in that arc would thus be described 'in via combusta'. Some of the older authorities gave its location as the last half of Libra and the whole of Capricorn; others, from Libra fifteen degrees to Scorpio fifteen degrees.

VIRGO AND MERCURY

Babylonia, Mesopotamia, and Assyria, declares Ptolemy in the *Tetrabiblos,* are familar to Virgo and Mercury, so that the study of mathematics and the observation of the five planets are special traits of these peoples.

VIRTUES OF THE HOURS

Among the ancient Aztecs of Mexico, particular properties and virtues were ascribed to the hours, the days, months, and the years.

VOX STELLARUM

This Latin title, which means *The Voice of the Stars,* was the name of an almanac which, under various editors, ran from the eighteenth century until late in the nineteenth.

WALLENSTEIN, ALBERT VON, DUKE OF FRIEDLAND

(1583-1634) Famous Austrian general. Died by assassination.
Noted for his interest in astrology, which he often mentions in
his correspondence.

WARBURG INSTITUTE

This institute in London University holds a collection of astrological matter gathered by Aby Warburg (died 1929) and his
colleague Fritz Saxl (died 1948). The collection consists of
medieval manuscripts treating of astrology, astrological symbolism, and papers and studies dealing with the more modern
concepts of astrological impacts and influences.

WATCHERS OF THE HEAVENS

This expression was applied by the Persians, about 3000 B.C.,
to the four Royal Stars, then to the angles of the zodiac: the
Watcher of the East; then at the vernal equinox — Aldebaran:
the Watcher of the North, which then marked the summer solstice — Regulus: the Watcher of the West, then at the autumnal
equinox — Antares: the Watcher of the South, which then
marked the winter solstice — Fomalhaut.

WATERLOO
Long before the Battle of Waterloo it was predicted, after consultation of the respective horoscopes of Napoleon and Wellington, that Napoleon would be defeated.

WATER SIGNS
These are Cancer, Pisces, Scorpio.

WHEEL OF PYTHAGORAS
A divinatory device for making forecasts by an arrangement of numbers that answered the questions proposed by the client.

WHOLE SIGNS
This expression applies to Gemini, Libra, Aquarius, and according to some astrologers, Taurus.

WIFE OF BATH
The wife of Bath, one of the characters in Geoffrey Chaucer's Canterbury Tales, recounts her erotic experiences and adds:
  Mine descendant is Tauro and Mars therein.

WILLIAM THE GOOD
King of Sicily (1152 - 1189) had an astrologer attached to his court.

WILL OF THE GODS
Among the ancient Babylonians and Sumerians there was a belief that the will of the gods, in relation to men's actions, could be deduced by observation of the movements of the planets and stars. Star-gazers, it was further thought, could read prospective disasters or good fortune in the varying aspects of the celestial bodies.

WISE MEN
To the early Christians, Jupiter, Saturn, and Mars symbolized the Three Wise Men from the East.

WOHL, LOUIS DE

Jewish Hungarian journalist and writer: well-known as an astrologer. Among other works, many of them fiction with a religious motif, he wrote *I Follow the Stars*.

WOODALE, JOHN

An eighteenth century English astrologer. Author of a treatise on astronomy and its relation to philosophy. He also published *The Nativity of Napoleon Bonaparte*.

YEATS, W. B.
(1865-1939) The Irish poet had astrological learnings and could cast his own horoscope.

YE LIU CHUTSAI
This Chinese scholar was the official astrologer attached to Genghis Khan (1162-1227), the famous Mongol conqueror, during all his Asian campaigns.

ZENITH
This term applies mathematically to the Pole of the Horizontal. The point directly overhead, through which pass the Prime Vertical and Meridian circles. Every place has its own zenith, and the nearer a planet is to the zenith, the more powerful is its influence. The expression is sometimes loosely applied to the cusp of the Tenth House, which strictly speaking is only the point of the zodiac or ecliptic path through which the meridian circles passes.

ZODIAC
A branch of the occult arts, the zodiacal involved the examination of the sky, the stars, the planets, the zodiacal signs, their relations to each other and their movements. All these were studied with mathematical precision in order to find what influences were exerted by the celestial bodies on the conduct and fate of man: when these influences were most potent or weakest.

The signs of the zodiac mark the twelve compartments of heaven. The six. northern signs are:

Aries	Cancer
Taurus	Leo
Gemini	Virgo

To each of these names was assigned a mystic symbol. The six southern signs are:

Libra	Capricorn
Scorpio	Aquarius
Sagittarius	Pisces

The zodiac was divided into two sections of Sun and Moon. Each half consists of six signs. The signs of the Moon of Night are: Aquarius, Pisces, Aries, Taurus, Gemini, Cancer. The signs of the Sun or Day are: Leo, Virgo, Libra, Scorpio, Sagittarius, Capricorn.

By means of scrupulous calculations the astrologer could determine the degree of influence exerted by the planets in relation to the zodiac. The issues to be determined astrologically concerned life; wealth; inheritance; land; wife, city, children, parents; health, sickness; marriage; death, religion, travel; honors, character; friends; enemies; captivity.

ZODIAC, MEANING OF
This astrological term is derived from *zoë*, the Greek word for life, and *diakos*, which denotes a wheel.

ZODIAC ASPECTS
Those measured in degrees along the Ecliptic. When used in connection with Primary Direction the Promittor's place is taken without latitude in contrast to the usual method used with mundane aspects wherein one takes cognizance of the latitude the significator will have when it arrives at the longitudinal degree at which the aspect is complete.

ZODIACAL DIRECTIONS
Those formed in the zodiac by the progressed motion of Ascendant, Midheaven, Sun, Moon, to aspects with the planets. These may be: Direct, in the order of the signs: or Converse, against the order of the signs.

ZODIACAL METALS
Zodiacal metals are those of the planetary Rulers, as follows:
Aries-Scorpio: Iron
Taurus-Libra: Copper
Gemini-Virgo: Mercury
Cancer: Silver
Leo: Gold
Sagittarius-Pisces: Tin
Capricorn-Aquarius: Lead

ZODIACAL PARALLELS
Any two points within the zodiac that are of equal declination are said to be in zodiacal parallel with each other. If both are North or both South declination they were anciently termed antiscions. Modern astrologers attribute astrological significance only to those points between two bodies in parallel on the same side of the equator.

ZODIACAL QUALITIES
The signs of the zodiac have individual properties and characteristics which reflect on human beings involved in astrological computations. Taurus, for instance, is feminine, cold, dry. Gemini is masculine, hot, moist. Cancer is feminine, nocturnal, cold. Leo is diurnal and bestial. Sagittarius is fiery and mutable. Virgo is earthy, quiet. Capricorn is earthy, solid. Libra is airy, restless. Aquarius is airy, inventive. Scorpio is secretive, passionate. Pisces is nervous, confused. Aries is creative, full of movement.

ZODIACAL SIGNS
The zodiacal signs and the planets are always present but not all of them are visible. Some lie above and others below the horizon. The antiquity of the study of the zodiacal signs is attested by the rock-painting near Cadiz and the maps of the heavens in stone-engravings in Galicia, Spain.

ZODIACAL SIGNS AND WEATHER
Ptolemy, in his *Tetrabiblos*, expounds the nature of the zodiacal signs and their effect on the weather.

ZODIAC AND CHARACTER

The signs of the zodiac are assumed to exert strong influence on personal traits, abilities, and potentialities. In a general sense, for instance, Aries is associated with mental ability. Taurus implies physical force. An adaptable nature is under the patronage of the Gemini. Cancer, on the other hand, stresses conservative tradition. Leo is exuberant and dominating. Virgo is critical. Libra is equated with justice. Daring men with initiative look toward Scorpio as their protector. Sagittarius denotes a dynamic personality. Intellectual capacity is conditioned by Capricorn. Humane traits belong to Aquarius, while a humble modesty hides behind Pisces.

ZODIAC AND PLANET

The twelve zodiacal signs are each considered to be under the direction of a particular planet: as the Sun, that rules the sign of Leo.

ZODIAC MAN

The Zodiac Man was a medieval representation of the human body in terms of the zodiacal signs, which were reproduced in the appropriate places on the body. The Zodiac Man, it was conceived, was totally under the guidance and dominance of the twelve signs.

ZODIACUS VITAE

This Latin expression means *the zodiac of life*. In astrology, it was an old school book by Marcellus Palingenius Stellatus that was first used in Shakespeare's day. The earliest edition extant, now in the British Museum, is dated 1574.

ZOROASTER

Persian founder of the cult of Zoroastrianism. He flourished approximately in the sixth century B.C. Zoroaster was a patron of astrological science and was knowledgeable with regard to its tenets and practices.